CONTENTS

"Repeat these basic essentials over and over to God's people. Warn them before God against pious nitpicking, which chips away at the faith. It just wears everyone out. Concentrate on doing your best for God, work you won't be ashamed of, laying out the truth plain and simple. Stay clear of pious talk that is only talk. Words are not mere words, you know. If they're not backed by a godly life, they accumulate as poison in the soul."

—2 Timothy 2:14–16 (MSG)

Concentrate and compete doing your best for God
From the sidelines, to the sidewalk, to significance

The Ripple Effect

To develop character
and spiritual formation

Bob Wilson

ISBN 978-1-64140-338-2 (paperback)
ISBN 978-1-64140-339-9 (digital)

Christian Faith Publishing, Inc.
832 Park Avenue
Meadville, PA 16335
www.christianfaithpublishing.com

Printed in the United States of America

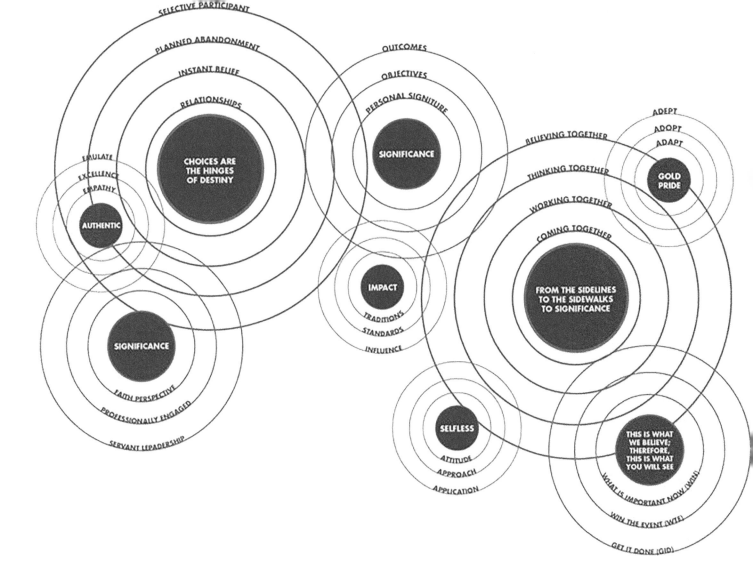

All of the above are phrases or triggers that remind a person what the appropriate action should be in response to a situation. Drop a pebble in the water and with a splash it is gone, but there is ripple circling that goes on and on. They keep spreading and spreading from the center and there is no way to stop them. Every idea, comment, lecture, song, act of kindness, hug, or smile has a ripple effect. The ripple effect is based on the concept that we are connected. We can and do affect each other. We influence each other in ways that are small and in ways that have a profound effect on our life. The result is a building of community that will affect how we treat others and that will have a ripple effect in the way we live our lives. We all become partners (teammates) for a greater purpose and it is up to each of us to find that purpose. All of us have passion for something as well as a vision and hope to use our gifts and talents for a greater purpose.

Introduction

In 2000, the NAIA introduced the Champions of Character Initiative to promote and develop character-driven athletics. Vanguard University made the unilateral decision with the inception of the Champions of Character Initiative that as an institution we would embrace the Champions of Character Program. This decision had support at the senior administrative level, the athletic administration level, our coaches, and our student athletes. Vanguard University is a leader in the NAIA Champions of Character Initiative.

The Champions of Character Initiative provided us, the Vanguard University Athletic Program, the opportunity to develop **GOLD PRIDE** for the continual character development and spiritual formation for the student athletes. **GOLD PRIDE** is the fundamental premise of the athletic program. The character class at Vanguard University was conceived and developed as a result of the institutions involvement and commitment to this initiative. The character class is taught each fall to all new student athletes. The class provides an opportunity to relate to the Vanguard University student athletes an application model for character-driven athletics in the context of a faith-based institution and how it can be modeled in representing Vanguard University as a student athlete from the sidelines (their sport) to the sidewalks (the community) to significance (a faith perspective for life).

The culture of the Vanguard University Athletic Program does more than lead with values; it seeks to bring those values alive for the student athletes and athletic staff. The **GOLD PRIDE** core values are the standards, values–rules of the road that hold

everyone accountable. The development of these standards needs to be intentionally formulated and articulated well so that the expectations of choices and behaviors are defined for what is important in the collegiate experience. The standards tell us how to treat other people, both inside and outside the team or community. Mike Krzyzewski once said, "You can be more flexible and in tune to what is important in the student athlete's world but not at the expense of compromising your values." We do not want confusion on what we believe to be the purpose-we want the student athletes to fully comprehend that purpose by hearing it, reading it, understanding it, competing with it, modeling it, and living it. In order to be a champion, you need to have the foundation of values that are worthy of being a champion.

GOLD PRIDE is presented through various mediums. We use various graphics, phrases, and triggers to help the student athletes remember, adhere to and follow the standards. The development of character and spiritual formation is an ongoing venture that is enhanced through team devotions, chapel presentations, Bible studies, and individual communication. Through this process, the student athletes will learn to understand how to strike and maintain a sense of balance in a world of our ever-shifting desire. They will no longer feel a need to justify their behavior, and they will develop a new respect for who they are as a person, student athlete, and teammate. We determine our own success, our destiny, by the standards we set and the choices we make. We hope that the student athletes utilize the freedom provided as a follower of Christ to adhere to the **GOLD PRIDE** standards.

GOLD PRIDE was selected for the following reasons: the school colors are navy and gold; gold is a precious metal highly esteemed for spiritual or moral quality. In addition, the highest award presented on the medal stand at the Olympics it is a gold medal. The Lions are the mascot and a family of lions is called a Pride; we believe we are family in the Athletic Program at Vanguard University and that we are better together.

This graphic symbolizes the essence of **GOLD PRIDE**. For every organization or program, it is important to keep the vision and mission in front of the team members, coaches, and student athletes. This vision is the heart of who we are. It defines who we are. A clearly communicated and understood vision empowers team members to work together for a higher purpose. We believe this graphic of the **GOLD PRIDE** triangle embraces this message.

The triangle represents the foundational premise of what Vanguard University Athletics is about. On each side of the triangle are our core covenants. The cornerstones of the **GOLD PRIDE** triangle are the core covenants of empathy, excellence, and emulate. These core covenants are guiding principles that need to be incorporated in the **GOLD PRIDE** initiative. A core covenant is a binding agreement where you will see action that is physically visible. Covenants are formed by design where each team member know what the covenants stand for; can articulate them and be committed to the vision and purpose of each covenant. The covenants establish what the team will compromise and what they will not compromise and the action of the covenants is reflected at all times win or lose. The three *Es* are what sets Vanguard University Athletics apart from others. **GOLD PRIDE** is all about being a part of a special group or team.

The foundational component of the Vanguard University Athletic Program is **Administrative Foundation**

1. Direction
   - This is the vision and leadership of the athletic program
   - "Let your light shine before all, so that they will see good things we do and praise your Father in heaven" (Mark 5:16).

2. Financial Stability
   - Athletic financial aid
   - Development of funding sources

3. Governance
   - Compliance with guidelines of NAIA
   - Compliance with guidelines of Golden State Athletic Conference

The developmental or productive component of the Vanguard University Athletic Program is the **Pursuit of Excellence**

1. Academic Excellence of the Student Athletes
   - The student athlete achieving their academic potential
   - Maintenance of a quality GPA for all student athletes
   - Graduation of student athletes equipped with an educational foundation for a career
   - Promotion of GSAC and NAIA Scholar Athletes

2. Athletic Excellence of Each Student Athlete and Their Teams
   - GSAC competition
     Top Tier (top 4) in the GSAC All Sports Award
   - Conference Championships
     Two conference championships per year
   - Directors Cup (National All Sports Competition)
     Top twenty-five NAIA school in the nation

3. Character Building
   - Developing Champions of Character student athletes a standard higher than victory
   - Development or enhancement of the student athletes spiritual foundation

The result or fulfillment component of the Vanguard University Athletic Program is Significance

1. *Significance* is when your primary *focus* is to achieve your objectives and the outcome of success occurs with your values intact.
2. The focus of significance is more than the normal measurement of success, it provides the following:
   o Faith perspective: A power to live on
      - Development of a life mission: What the student athlete believes God wants them to do with their life.
      - Christ as the center of their life
   o Professionally engaged: A purpose to live for
      - Development of a vision: "Where there is no vision the people are unrestrained—there is no purpose—nor reason to perform" (Proverbs 29:18).
      - Accept responsibility for developing themselves and career

   o Servant Leadership: People to live for (relationships)
      - Relationships provide us with the challenges, encouragement, and comfort we need

3. *Significance* seeks enduring results
4. *Significance* doing the right thing, right the right way.
5. *Significance* is necessary to become an *ultimate competitor*

A few years ago, I was talking with a parent of a college-age student athlete and the parent made this statement, "My son told me he is going to college to find himself." The Father's response was, "I did not know he was lost." To be a student athlete in college is a unique and valuable opportunity. Many college-age people do not take advantage of their collegiate years to grow. They want to be successful but are reluctant to think about what they need to do to develop their gifts and talents, learn new skills, and broaden their abilities so their quality of life is enhanced and improved. They are only willing to grow enough to accommodate their current situation or problems; instead they need to grow enough to achieve their true potential. The most important relationship you will ever have is with yourself. You choose what happens to you. Your choices reflect who you are, your character. Your decisions determine your destiny. Are you doing your best to fully accept that responsibility? Your behavior is a product of your conscious thought based on your values, purpose, and vision.

The *Ripple Effect in Character Development and Spiritual Formation* is a holistic, integrated process intended to provide each individual the opportunity for individual internal assessment and review that aid in the establishment of values and principles that will be seen in behavioral patterns that lead to significance. *The Ripple Effect to Develop Character and Spiritual Formation* manual is a resource that provides information and instruction for you to reach significance in your life. *The Ripple Effect* manual is designed to provide a guide that can apply to anyone who has an interest in becoming more empathetic, desiring to pursue excellence that emulates Christ and it will allow you to be more effective and efficient. It is an application model that is founded on Christian values and principles with the use of athletic jargon especially for the student athlete.

The Prayer of Jabez

He was the one who prayed to the God of Israel, "Oh that you would bless me and expand my territory! Please be with me in all that I do, and keep me from all trouble and pain!" And God granted him his request (1 Chronicles 4:10). Jabez was born into the tribe of Judah and eventually became the notable head of the clan. His story begins with his name. His mother called his name Jabez because she bore him in pain. Does this sound like a start to a promising life? All babies arrive with a certain amount of pain, but something about Jabez's birth went beyond the usual, so much so that his mother chose to memorialize it in her son's name. Only God knows for sure what caused

the pain of this anguished mother. Yet by far the heaviest burden of Jabez's name was how it defined his future. Despite his dismal prospects, Jabez found a way out. He had grown up hearing about the God of Israel who had freed his forefathers from slavery, rescued them from powerful enemies, and established them in a land of plenty. By the time he was an adult, Jabez believed and fervently hoped in this God of miracles and new beginnings.

You may not have the focus or spiritual formation at this time to be able to pray as boldly as Jabez. Everyone is at different stages in their relationship with Christ. *The ripple effect* allows you to explore the influence or impact of Christ's blessing as an ultimate value in your life so you begin to understand what Christ is attempting to do in you, through you, and around you for His glory. Being a Christian student athlete is not about religion, rules, regulations, or rituals; it is about a relationship you have with Christ as Jabez did.

The journey through *The Ripple Effect* manual needs to begin by claiming this statement:

> **I might not be where I want to be, I may not be where
> I ought to be, but I am not where
> I used to be, and by
> God's grace I commit to being
> on my way to develop a stronger
> character and spiritual formation
> so I can be where I should be.**

A poem by Sharon Jordan expresses the ripple effect well.

The Ripple Effect

Life sometimes seems
So short
That it existed
Only in our dreams
But just like the stone
Thrown upon the pond
The ripples and influence
Reach far beyond
One life can touch those
Whom she or he never knew
In special ways
Which bring hope and renew
Our belief that life
Always has meaning
Whether short or long
It's all in believing

Through the use of this phrase, it is our desire that the lens of how student athletes view their collegiate experience will be enhanced.

FROM THE SIDELINE - TO THE SIDEWALK - TO SIGNIFICANCE

The sideline represents their given sport, their teammates and coaches and the lesson that they learn that are inherent to their sport. The sidewalks represent the community, both the athletic community and the community at large which includes both on and off campus. Significance represents the continued destination of their journey. Jesus' goal is to save souls, our goal is to provide the opportunity for each student athlete to develop the character qualities of Christ through their spiritual formation so their choices, behavior and decisions lead them to significance and they become an influencer or role model through their athletic participation as an ultimate competitor and a person that has an impact during their lifetime as a parent, husband/wife, in their career and in their place of worship.

THE RIPPLE EFFECT

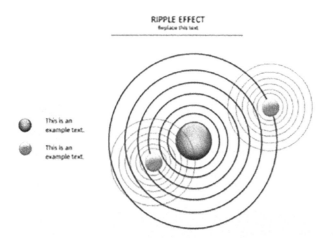

The format of *The Ripple Effect* manual is that in each section there is a message (the pebble), theme (the ripple effect), and an action or application (the impact) that you can use to develop and improve your character and spiritual formation.

Section	Message (Pebble)	Theme (Ripple Effect)	Action or Application (Impact)
I	Who can you become	The ripple effect What is the Ultimate Competitor	Begin with the end in mind
II	You can become more than you have become	The five *P*s	Who Am I (sense of self) Whose Am I (sense of self in Christ)
III	The rules of the road	Fist two Commandments/ Live 5 core values	Live 5 Core Values Defined
IV	The culture we create permeates everything we touch	Coming together Working together Thinking together Believing together	Establishing and defining **GOLD PRIDE**
V	Better together	Relationships/Teammate/Team	Ownership of **GOLD PRIDE**
VI	Look what you have become	Role Model/Authentic Leader/Christian Athlete/Ultimate Competitor	Audience of One

Each ripple effect will be discussed and presented separately but the circle of the ripples will interlock in the development of character and spiritual formation. To be able to fully reach significance you must have a solid working knowledge of each section (ripple), understand the message of each and put the theme into practice, and make application for the full impact of the ripple effect to occur.

To define, model, shape, and reinforce the character development and spiritual formation we use triggers in the form of graphics, phrases, and acronyms to aid in developing strong character habits. A trigger is a set of words or an image that reminds a person what the appropriate action should be in response to a situation. As the student athletes hear, read, study, and discuss the concepts, terms, and phrases provided in this manual the hope that these values and principles have significant meaning for each student athlete during their collegiate experience and they begin to model them as a quality Christian student athlete.

In athletics, the "stat sheet" is a valuable tool to assess your performance. At the end of each section will be a "stat sheet" of individual growth exercises that will provide an opportunity for you to apply the concepts presented.

1. **Fundamentals: Basic Skills**
    *   How many times have you heard a coach tell you that you need to improve on your fundamentals if you are going to improve your game? This will be a review of the key fundamentals in each section to make sure you have the basic skills down.

2. **Strength and Conditioning Training: Improving Your Shape**
    *   To be a quality student athlete you need to be in quality con-dition. These exercises are to be used to build your strength and conditioning in a particular area just as you build your body with cardio vascular endurance and weight training.
    *   By applying these exercises you have an opportunity to improve on your fundamentals to become better.

3. **Game Day: Performing with Excellence**
    *   Have you worked hard enough on your strength and condition, and fundamentals to perform when the lights are on?

**"I was walking in the park and this guy waved at me.
Then he said, I am sorry, I thought you were someone else. 'I said, I am'"
(Demetri Martin).**

A Winning Attitude

When Jordan Davidson first arrived at Vanguard University on a scholarship to play soccer, she recalls that many of the people who met her came away with the impression that she was not particularly interested in making friends. At the time, she did not have the relationship with God that she does now, and she felt uncomfortable in the environment at Vanguard. "I didn't know who God was," she says. "I didn't like it here, and I wanted to go home."

It wasn't until Jordan began the class called Champions of Character, a requirement for all Vanguard athletes, that her heart began to be transformed by God through careful mentorship. Her group leader in the class was Brian "Boomer" Roberts, an assistant coach for the men's basketball team. As Jordan began confronting her discomfort and asking challenging questions about the nature of Christian faith, Boomer patiently guided her to an understanding of God's truth and power. She gave her life to Christ, and a truer version of herself emerged. "Boomer brought me in and walked with me," says Jordan. "And when I gave my life to Christ, things rapidly started to change for me. I became a nicer, better, and more joyful person. Now, everyone is surprised to hear how 'mean' I was."

Jordan's transformation had a powerful effect on her soccer career as well. She recommitted herself to excellence on the field, and in her junior year, she won the GSAC Player of the Year award. She treasured this symbol of how her hard work and talent had paid off, but it came with some added difficulties in her senior year. She discovered that she was a marked player: each opponent devoted special attention to shutting down her game. Jordan responded by striving to do whatever she could within her limited opportunities to help her team win, and this attitude was fruitful as well. She won GSAC Player of the Year again in her senior year. "That was such a humbling moment," she recalls. "I just wanted my team to do well, and it was such

an honor to have my efforts recognized like that."

Jordan's successful season reinforces the attitude that prevails in Vanguard's athletics programs. "It's very competitive," says Jordan. "And everyone contributes in different ways. Even if you're not playing a lot, your identity is not just in your sport." The support Vanguard athletes give each other in this regard is also crucial. "Everyone wants everyone else to do well," explains Jordan. "No player is left behind."

Jordan discovered that the larger academic and social community of Vanguard she and her fellow athletes are situated in is also one of loyalty and encouragement. During her junior year, a family emergency obligated her to immediately fly home to Arizona in the middle of the semester. Coaches, professors, and students alike rose up around Jordan, ameliorating the disruption that her circumstances caused in her life and reminding her of the power of God's love as it's expressed in community. "Everyone—not just my soccer team—reached out and prayed for me," she recalls. "That support helped me get through that time in my life. It's unique to be around people who care. I am so thankful to be at Vanguard."

A Season of Significance

With a little under four minutes left in the 2014 NAIA Division I Basketball National Championship game, a pair of Emmanuel College free throws put them just two points down from Vanguard University, who had led for most of the game. The situation called for some heroics from Vanguard's

First Team All-American Preston Wynne, and he did not fail to deliver. Wynne hit a baseline fadeaway while being fouled, putting Vanguard back up by a comfortable margin and leading the Lions to its first-ever NAIA Men's Division I Basketball National Championship with a 70–65 win.

Along the way, Preston Wynne picked up a number of other awards. He received the tournament's MVP award, a place on the NAIA's All-Tournament team, and was also selected as the Golden State Athletic Conference's (GSAC) Player of the Year. However, for Wynne, his season amounted to so much more than personal accolades. In an interview with Indian Country Today, Wynne explained, "For me, awards are not really that great. It's more the experience than the award. The award doesn't say to me the best player. It says a great experience." And as for that experience, Wynne made it clear that playing at Vanguard was special. "It's an amazing place," he said. "We have one of the smallest gyms in the country and almost every student would pack that gym every night. It was just an amazing, amazing experience. It's a family atmosphere you get when you come down here."

The win in the national championship game capped off a season of enormous accomplishment for Vanguard's men's basketball team, which was recently honored for its success by the Orange County Board of Supervisors. The team finished with a school-best 32–6 record and also won the Golden State Athletic Conference (GSAC) regular season and tournament titles. Vanguard University head basketball coach Rhett Soliday was named the NAIA's National Coach of the Year, but in interviews

after the game, he kept his focus on more intangible achievements. "It feels amazing," he said. "We just praise God. We said before this game, win or lose, that we're going to give Him the glory, because He made this a special season. Our guys believed from day one. They have a strong faith in each other."

A week after the title game, Vanguard hosted a rally called "A Season of Significance," which gave the community an opportunity to celebrate the excellence of the women's basketball team in addition to the men's team. Vanguard's women spent their entire undefeated season ranked number one en route to the GSAC Championship, coach Russ Davis won his third NAIA Coach of the Year, and point guard Nicole Ballestero received NAIA Player of the Year honors.

Students, faculty, staff, alumni, and supporters packed The Pit for the rally, where various coaches, athletic staff, and Vanguard president Michael Beals gave short speeches thanking the individuals who supported the teams along the way. In his introduction, MC Ed Arnold talked about the teams being more than just excellent basketball players. "Character-wise and otherwise these are outstanding people," he said. In his closing remarks, President Beals congratulated the men's team and assured them that throughout the rest of Vanguard's existence their banner would remain on the wall of whatever gym facility Vanguard has. President Beals also gave an encouraging word for students to cultivate their God-given talents, whatever they may be, like the members of the men's and women's teams had cultivated their athletic talents.

Back on the Court

After her junior season as one of the leaders on Vanguard University's women's basketball team, Riley Holsinger received a personal letter of support from a seemingly unlikely source: a competitor from another collegiate basketball team. The letter said in part:

"I just wanted to let you know that my team and I have been and will be praying for you. Injuries are not easy, but I pray that the Lord can use this trial in your life to draw you nearer to Him and grow your faith. And I pray that you will continue to press on and trust Him, knowing that you can rejoice in suffering because the Lord will use it for good. [. . .] We are told in several places that we can trust in Him through trials and we can rely on His grace to sustain us and persevere through any season we may face. [. . .] Stay strong, girl. You are a very respected player and leader, and I can't wait to see you fully recovered and back on the court."

This word of encouragement came from an athlete at The Master's College, and it was particularly precious to Riley, because she received it after suffering one of the most devastating injuries an athlete can face. Near the end of a spectacular season, that would see her awarded a NAIA First Team All-America selection, rank fifth nationally in scoring, and win the GSAC Player of the Year, Riley tore the ACL in her right knee. The injury requires months of difficult rehabilitation, and as Riley faces the challenge of getting back on the court, she has been lifted up by the prayer and support of Vanguard's close-knit community of coaches and athletes.

"The most important thing I have learned while being here at Vanguard as a student athlete is how important it is to keep God first in all that I do," says Riley. "I have learned the importance of prayer. Given my injury, I could not have gotten over the hurdles I encountered without the prayers of my teammates, coaches, friends, and family."

Recognizing the distress and vulnerability that can accompany a major injury, coaches from every athletic team in the school reached out to make sure that Riley was recuperating physically and emotionally, treating Riley as a whole person, not just as a ballplayer. "The community here at Vanguard and throughout the GSAC Conference gave me so much encouragement and support, and for that I am grateful," says Riley. "The coaches here are supportive and loving. They not only care about us as athletes, but as individuals off the court."

Riley's greatest support came from her closest allies: the women's basketball team. The culture of relationship established and modeled by the coaches at Vanguard permeates the teams completely. "My basketball team is unique because we are more than just sisters," says Riley. "We are extremely close. My team provided me with unconditional love and support before, during, and after my injury. I can never repay them for that, and I really do hope they know how much I appreciate them. They are such a blessing in my life."

Riley and her teammates are strong competitors and very aware of the legacy of success the women's basketball team at Vanguard represents. They approach every game with the same level of intensity and strive to improve after losses. This strong athletic success resides in the context of and is empowered by the relentless focus on values articulated in the Champions of Character program at Vanguard. To Riley, this is one of the most important facets of the Vanguard experience. "My favorite class at Vanguard has been the Champions of Character class," she says. "It really helped me come out of my comfort zone. I learned so much about what I value most and what we value here at Vanguard as student athletes."

This emphasis on values is what sets Vanguard apart, and Riley's personal experience stands as a testament, still in progress, of how suffering can be used powerfully by God for His good work. "Vanguard's athletic department separates itself from other athletic departments because of the strong family relationship it shares," she says. "Everyone here in the athletic department is a brother and sister to one another. The Christian community is the foundation of our athletic department, and I believe it is why we all continue to thrive."

" THE VANGUARD ATHLETIC PROGRAM HAS REALLY IMPACTED MY LIFE AND THE LIVES OF MY TEAMMATES. NOT ONLY DO OUR OWN COACHES CARE ABOUT US, BUT COACHES FROM OTHER TEAMS INVEST INTO OUR LIVES AS WELL. THERE IS A CLEAR PASSION FOR PLAYING THE GAME AND WINNING, BUT THEY GO BEYOND THAT. IT IS A REAL PRIVILEGE PLAYING FOR AN ATHLETIC PROGRAM THAT HELPS US GROW SPIRITUALLY AND WITH INTEGRITY.

- MEGAN HILL '14
SOCCER

The Ripple Effect manual can become a source of encouragement, inspiration, and development for those that invest and apply the values and principles presented. It can be a great ride where there is no finish line.

Your decision to use *The Ripple Effect* to enhance your character development and spiritual formation may be the most important choice you have ever made. The most important relationship you will ever have is with yourself. Our hope is that you will choose to embrace the challenge of becoming more than who you have become, invest in and take ownership of **GOLD PRIDE** and pursue excellence academically, athletically, and in building the character qualities of Christ. Welcome aboard.

Stat Sheet

Fundamentals: Basic Skills

1. Review the chart of the ripple effect and relate how the circle of ripples will interlock in the development of your character and spiritual formation. How are they dependent on each other?

Strength and Conditioning Training: Improving Your Shape

1. Who is Jabez and what significance does he have in your character development and spiritual formation?

Game Day: Performing with Excellence

1. *The Ripple Effect to Develop Character and Spiritual Formation* allows you to grow and mature as a person. Jesus's goal is to save souls, what is our goal?

Who Can
You Become

The Ripple Effect **Begin with the End in Mind**

"Pieces"
by Meredith Andrews

It's a complex puzzle you call your life
It's an uphill climb, it's a constant fight
And it wears you down
Feeling like you're alone,
like you don't belong
And you won't be loved if
you don't measure up
And you wear your scars
Like they're who you are
Give Him your wounds, your
bruised and broken pieces
All your questions, all your secrets
You don't have to hide who you are
You belong to someone greater
Than all your past mistakes and failures
Rested who He is
He knows how to make your pieces fit
He's the light on the road when
you're lost in the dark

And He won't run away if
you show your heart
Wants you to believe it
You can taste that freedom
When you give Him your wounds,
your bruised and broken pieces
All your questions, all your secrets
You don't have to hide who you are
You belong to someone greater
Than all your past mistakes and failures
Rested who He is
He knows how to make your pieces fit
You are completely known
You are completely loved
This is where you belong

"The secret to growth in character and spiritual formation is continual evaluation and assessment. Test yourselves to make sure you are solid in the faith. Don't drift along taking everything for granted. Give yourselves regular checkups. You need firsthand evidence, not mere hearsay that Jesus Christ is in you. Test it out. If you fail the test, do something about it." (2 Corinthians 13:5)

Who Can You Become

Be careful how you speak to yourself;
Be careful how you think of yourself;
Be careful of how you conduct yourself;
Be careful of how you develop yourself.
—Tony Dungy

Mark Twain once said, "The two most important days in your life are the day you were born and the day you figure out why."

If you want something you have never had before, you must be willing to do something you have never done before.

The concepts presented in Stephen Covey's book, *The 7 Habits of Highly Effective People* provides a context to organize the approach that is used in *The Ripple Effect*. The habits are incorporated in the following manner:

Be proactive: This is the intentionality of *The Ripple Effect*. We have developed an interactive curriculum that allows you as a student athlete to have a better understanding of who you are as a person and how that relates to who you are as a student athlete. We define expectations, model values, reinforce behavior, and reward examples of **GOLD PRIDE**. The approach helps student athletes' to be cognizant of relationships in hopes that they will become a better and more empathic teammate which leads to their ability to become an ultimate competitor.

Begin with the end in mind: The phrase, from the sidelines to the sidewalks to sig-nificance, allows us to work with each student athlete in an attempt to use their collegiate athletic experience to help them be a role model (influencer) in their community and leads to significance (a faith perspective—professional engaged in a career of their choice—becoming a servant leader, an understanding of the importance of giving back).

Put first things first: It is the hope that each student athlete will be able to prioritize their passions that will lead them to be more effective and efficient making choices that will enhance their performance both in athletics (sidelines) and in life (sidewalks).

Think win-win: This is the pursuit of excellence (academically, athletically, and in building the character qualities of Christ) through developing their skills, quality relationship, and enhancing their ability to become a better person, an ultimate teammate and competitor.

Seek first to understand, then to be understood: The development of empathy, which is the building block for successful relationships.

Synergy: The value of learning to serve others (to become selfless). Serving others is empathy and excellence put into acts and action. This is being part of something bigger than yourself.

Sharpening the saw: Developing the spiritual formation where there is a realization that God made you to be you. Jesus wants you to use your gifts and talents for His glory.

An expectation is a belief about what might happen in the future. If you have great expectations, you think something good will come your way. Many people, however, keep their expectations low and in that way they do not risk being disappointed. "You will always rise to the level of the expectations you have for yourself, but will never be able to rise above the imaginary ceiling you construct in your mind. Your expectations will also be affected by how much you allow the things around you to affect the direction of your journey. The key is to continue your thoughts on where you want to go, regardless of those distractions. What do you want your tomorrow to look like? Allow your mind and your heart to embrace that direction."[1] Carl Jung once stated, "Your vision will become clear only when you look into your heart . . . He who looks outside, dreams. He, who looks inside, awakens." "When you discover 'what you want' you get 'who you are' thrown in. What you truly want will derive from who you really are. In other words, it will tap into your personality, your skill set, and your passion."[2]

Perceptions are built by a lot of things: reputation, other people's portrayals, sometimes even past performance. Uncovering reality sometimes requires a little work. The first step in developing a good game plan is to determine who you really are—or should be—beyond the perceptions of the world and beyond the lure of whom society says you should be.[3]

Character growth and your spiritual formation do not come from rules but from small actions of responsibility that occur daily. It is more important to pursue the hard right instead of the easy wrong. When it is all said and done, your reputation does not matter. It is important, but what others think of you is simply out of your control. What does matter, however, is what you think of yourself. Your integrity, that is something you can control.[4] Every day you are faced with challenges and the temptation to conform. But God made you with unique gifts and characteristics, and being a positive role model starts with being yourself. You were created for a reason. It does not matter what you missed or how you may have messed up; the fact is that your future is ahead of you. What will you do with it?[5]

Paul in 2 Corinthians 12:7–10 provides this thought-provoking advice, "Everyone was created by God and in the image of God. God created you to be you with all your strengths and limitations. Somebody pointing out your limitations, real or otherwise, does not change your strengths or the truth that you are who you are and the fact that you will always remain a child of God. Because of the extravagance of those revelations, and so I would not get a big head, I was given the gift of a handicap to keep me in constant touch with my limitations. Satan's angel did his best to get me down; what he in fact did was push me to my knees. No danger then of walking around high and mighty! At first I did not think of it as a gift, and begged God to remove it. Three times I did that, and then He told me,

My grace is enough; it's all you need.
My strength comes into its
own in your weakness.

Once I heard that, I was glad to let it happen. I quit focusing on the handicap and began appreciating the gift. It was a case of Christ's strength moving in on my weakness. Now I take limitations in stride, and with good cheer, these limitations that cut me down to size— abuse, accidents, opposition, bad breaks. I just let Christ take over! And so the weaker I get, the stronger I become."

Everyone feels pressured to tie their personal value to their sport, their environment, their status. Paul talks about the fruits of the spirit in Galatians 5:22–23: "love, joy, peace, patients, kindness, goodness, faithfulness, gentleness, and self-control." Yet we rarely embrace these inner qualities because they do not seem to fit within the world of competitive athletics.

Writing about the power of the tongue, James in the New Testament notes that both fresh and salt water cannot flow from the same spring. "What is down in the well will come up in the bucket."[6] What is down in your well? From what source does the water in your well come? From where do you draw strength and direction in your life? Whatever is there will govern you thoughts for today and tomorrow. Fill it well.[7]

Isaiah 55:1–2 says, "All of you who are thirsty, come to me and drink! And to those of you who do not have money to buy food, come and eat for free! Why do you spend your money on something that is not real food and does not really satisfy you? Come to me and you will eat what is good; your soul will enjoy the stuff that really satisfies!"

What you feel and what is real are not the same. Whatever you are hungry for determines your destiny. Your appetite is influenced by your associations. "Shifting your priorities will require some changes in your life, but in the end it will be more than worth it."[8] "A life centered on Christ, one that 'chases after God' will not only help

free you from being preoccupied with your success, your position on the team, and your current situation—but it also will redirect your focus so that you can learn to embrace the priorities that truly matter."[9] In doing so you become authentic which requires letting go of who you think you should be and embracing who God wants you to be.

The Ultimate Competitor

Jesus Christ is the greatest competitor that ever lived.

"In a race, all runners run to win the prize, Therefore run in such a way as to win"

When sports fans get together sometimes they debate who they feel is the greatest of all competitors. A number of publications and media outlets published their list of the Top 100 Athletes each year. Many people were outraged that their favorite sports hero was not mentioned or did not rank as high as they thought they should be.

Many of us define a true competitor as a champion—one who is strong and mighty, one who overcomes adversity, always prevails and claims victory. History is filled with competitors like this. But there is only one Ultimate Competitor. His name is Jesus Christ.

Those who compete well compete for an audience of one; they compete with the cross. The vertical part of the cross represents an open line to Jesus allowing you to use your gifts and talents to honor Him in competition. The horizontal part of the cross represents His love for us as He stretches out His arms wide to indicate how much He loves us, the ultimate sacrifice; as you embrace that love you indicate how much you love Christ and demonstrate that because He was selfless for you, you can become selfless in Him and thus you become something bigger than yourself. Jesus's mission was to save souls; our mission is to acquire Christ-like character to model at all times especially in competition.

To become an Ultimate Competitor you need to emulate *Christ* in competition. The acronym of **CHRIST** effectively describes and defines these competitive qualities.

COLLABORATION
HUMILITY
RISILIENT
INVESTED
STRENGTH
TRUTH

Christ selected and taught twelve ordinary men that He used in an extraordinary manner. While Christ was on earth, His twelve followers were called disciples. The word "disciple" refers to a learner or follower. The disciples followed Jesus Christ, learned from Him, and were trained by Him. In the same manner, Christ has left a footprint for you to learn to become an Ultimate Competitor. You need to identify and understand how collaboration, humility, resiliency, investment, strength, and truth depict Christ as an Ultimate Competitor.

Collaboration

Collaboration relies on openness and sharing knowledge, as well as a significant level of focus and accountability. Christ was a collaborative leader who intentionally and skillfully managed relationship that enabled His disciples to succeed individually while accomplishing a collective purpose. Competition requires many different types of challenges. A collaborative team works together aggressively for a purpose.

Major components of collaboration are **compatibility and cooperation**. **Compatibility** is the ability to exist and perform together in harmony as Christ did with His disciples. Christ was committed to His team—the disciples. He was relentless in His pursuit. He took ownership of His purpose and cause, team values, and His teammates and thus, they were teachable and there was shared the joy of the inner circle. His commitment was displayed in His actions and He always did more than was necessary.

Cooperation is an act working together for a common purpose or benefit in all levels of a team. Christ listened and related to each team member to find the best way to accomplish things as opposed to having His own way. When improvement was needed He looked first at Himself and therefore, the team was further developed through His selfless sacrifice.

Humility

A basic definition uses many times in this document is that humility is not thinking less of you, but thinking of others instead and acting in their best interest, instead of your own. The Bible illustrates humility as a quality of being courteously respectful of others. It is the opposite of arrogance and vanity. Instead for the "me first attitude" humility says, "you first."

True humility is when someone sees what is needed and steps forward. Jesus did not withhold Himself. He stepped forward to meet the needs of humanity at a great cost to Himself. He was present in times of need. He spoke boldly at times and remained silent at others. He was willing to confront what needed to be confronted rather than being concerned about Himself.

Humility was one of Christ's exceptional qualities. This quality was fostered through His **competence and character**. **Competence** is the ability to do something successfully and efficiently. Christ was able to perform with excellence because His approach was the same in every situation. He had the ability to communicate and relate with His teammates, as well as the ability to motivate them to perform to their potential. He had an inner strength that allowed Him to aggressively lead; He always displayed a quiet confidence which allowed Him to build trust with His teammates.

Character is a combination of mental characteristics and behavior that distinguishes a person or group. Christ demonstrated a strong will. Call it heart, courage, or will, competitors have the ability and desire to leave their handprints on everything important in their life. Having desire is one thing, being able to impose your desire and resolve into action so strong that it impacts everything around you is another. Christ accomplished this because He had integrity; integrity is the value you place on

yourself—maturity, which is the balance between being courageous and considerate, and His belief of abundant mentality, that on His team everyone has a role and that all roles are important for success.

Even though Christ was extremely competent, His character qualities allowed Him to be humble because He did not require or expect special treatment. He performed and displayed His effectiveness with a sense of dignity and provided us with an example of humility and that separates Him from all other leaders and Ultimate Competitors.

Resilient

Resilience is the capacity to withstand stress and adversity. Psychologists have long recognized the capabilities of humans to adapt and overcome risk and adversity. Being resilient does not mean going through life without experiencing stress and pain. People feel a range of emotions after adversity and loss. The road to resilience lies in working through the emotions and effects of stress and painful events. Resilient people decide that somehow, some way, they will do the very best they can to survive, cope, and make things turn out well. They expect to bounce back. Call it grit, hardiness, fortitude, or inner strength—by whatever name, it is not so much your experience or training, it's your level of resilience in the face of stress that determines whether you succeed or fail.

Jesus was a role model of resilience, courage, and comfort to others in His darkest hour of physical agony and spiritual separation from His Heavenly Father. Resilience is the most difficult trait to emulate in becoming an Ultimate Competitor. Athletic traits that allow you to develop more resilience are **courage and creativeness**.

Courage is mental or moral strength to venture, persevere, and withstand danger, fear, or difficulty. A person that is capable of accepting and embracing discipline increases their ability to be courageous, stay focused to the task at hand as well as stay with their commitments in difficult times. This discipline, commitment, and attention are expressed in their love for the game in which they participate. A person who demonstrates courage does so through an expression of the heart.

Creativeness is one's ability or power to create. To overcome adversity and be resilient, you need to be able to start your own engine, show initiative and are not dependent or require special treatment from your coach or teammates. Your focus is used to put forth a greater effort in your work habits and in your preparation. As your work ethic and preparation for your sport returns, your passion for the team and the activity is renewed and enhanced.

Invested

Investing is giving yourself to a purpose greater than yourself, devoting your time, effort, and energy to a particular purpose or cause with the expectation there will be a worthwhile result. Christ lived by a standard that enhanced the people around Him. His investment rose above the call. During His time with the disciples as well as now Christ was an example in His speech, His conduct and behavior, His love and His faith. All of us need to identify areas in our life where we can accomplish more by investing ourselves.

Christ made the most of His opportunities. Greatness is not a matter of talent but of choices you make. The question is, are you willing to make the *competitive commitment* to become more authentic by letting go who you think you should be and embracing who God believe you can become?

As the Ultimate Competitor Christ lived in and loved the moment. **Competitive** is defined as having a strong desire to succeed. Christ was at His best when His best was needed. He had a singleness of purpose and an intensity level that others did not. He had the capacity to stay focused with the task at hand even through difficult challenges.

Commitment is the state or quality of being dedicated to a cause, purpose, or activity. It entails staying with obligations and promises. Commitment is maybe the most important building block of true competitiveness. Showing up every day is not enough to demonstrate commitment, you need to be totally "locked in" to what you are doing when you show up—that is commitment. Do not mistake routine for commitment. In the army they use a phrase "adapt and overcome." It is a phase born out of commitment. No matter what the situation, a solider was expected to use all available resources—both internal and external—to adapt to the situation, work the problem, and overcome any obstacle to complete the mission.[10] It is a commitment to continuous improvement of your covenants. This mind set allows you to compete fearlessly. During competition you continually remaining aggressively and play to win rather than playing to avoid failing.

Strength

What does it mean to be strong? Is it someone who comes off as confident, someone who is comfortable in their own skin, or perhaps someone who can take on the world? Christ would in some respect meet all of these. For the purpose of depicting Christ as an Ultimate Competitor strength is defined as having a great capacity to face challenges, having the mental skills (inner strength) and physical capabilities to confront difficulties of all kinds. When a person is strong-minded, they have the energy and stamina to face a challenge without being robbed of inner strength. Inner strength is an expression of willpower. Its presence or lack determines whether you are assertive or not, preserving or not, whether you will fail or accomplish goals.

Vital values that enhance your inner strength are *cognitive* **thought** and developing into a *complete* person. Without them, it is difficult to start anything and difficult to get to the finish line and finish what you started.

Cognitive **thought** is relating to, being, or involving conscious intellectual activity (as thinking, reasoning, or remembering). The athletic expression for this trait is termed mental toughness. Mental toughness is an inner strength that allow you to control emotional responses and concentrate on what has to be done in pressure situations; you use emotion and energy to make yourself tougher, not to give your opponents strength; nothing can happen that will break your spirit, you stay enthusiastic, confident, and positive. This allows you to play within yourself, to play smart. Mental toughness is the combination of discipline and the strength of your will. The competitor in Christ refused to allow His spirit to be broken. In the athletic arena, there will be pressure. Pressure does not change the competitor; they have prepared themselves to be stable, poised, and energized by the heightened intensity.

Complete is having all the required or customary characteristics, skills to pursue excellence. This would include being accountable for your action, being part of the solution and not part of the problem when adversity surfaces; it entails pursuing excellence in all areas of your life not just in the athletic arena. A complete person has the ability to control the things that are controllable. They know that they do not have the capacity to control the opponent's preparation or behavior, referee calls, and the weather. Therefore, their entire focus is on the things they can control, which is their preparation, their approach, and their attitude. They have learned to separate their performance from the outcome. They are responsible for preparation and effort, God is responsible for outcome.

Truth

Truth is defined as the real facts about something: the things that are true, the quality or state of being true, a statement or idea that is true or accepted as true. Truth is far more than facts. It is not just something we act upon. It acts upon us. We cannot change the truth, but the truth can change us. Randy Alcorn of Eternal Perspective Ministries relates these thoughts about Jesus and the truth; Jesus says, "I am the way, the truth and the life; no man comes to the Father but by Me" He did not say He would show the truth or teach the truth or model the truth. He is the truth. He is the source of all truth, the embodiment of truth and therefore the reference point for evaluating all truth-claims." Rick Warren in his comments about Christ and the truth says, "He does not say truth is a religion or a ritual or a set of rules and regulations. He says "I."

Truth is a person. Truth is not a principle. Truth is a person: Jesus Christ.

Consistent is adhering to the same principles and purpose—in other words, the truth. Consistency describes the life of Christ. Jesus models for you, the competitor, a quiet confidence that demonstrates self-discipline, reliability, poise, and self-control.

Christ displayed the consistency of the truth through His love. He was a compassionate person. ***Compassion*** is someone who demonstrates kindness, caring, and a willingness to help others. A compassionate competitor will sacrifice personal interests of glory for the welfare of all. This put the proper perspective on competition; it limits people pleasing, reduces human expectation on you as a competitor, and focuses you on the expectation of Christ and not on your performance. You display moral courage because you demonstrate the ability to compete without compromising yourself or your character and to compete for Christ the Ultimate Competitor. Thus, allowing your identity as an ultimate com-

petitor to be on the cross competing for an audience of one.

The root word of "competition" is the Latin word "petere," which means to search or strive for. Most often is it used in the context of striving or searching for something of value or excellence. The preposition "com" means together. So literally, competition can be defined as a mutual quest or striving for excellence. It is more process-oriented than outcome-oriented. Competitors strive together or with each other to bring out the best by presenting a worthy challenge. Competition, therefore, is not defined by winning and losing, but by the degree to which all competitors realize their fullest potential. Since true competition is a "mutual quest for excellence" there are no winners or losers; everyone who competes wins. This cooperative sense of competition is a value-driven process that leads to respect for others—your teammates and your opponent, personal and team integrity, being the best you are capable of becoming instead of, doing whatever it takes to get ahead and win. Your self-worth is never determined by winning or losing. Our desire to dominate an opponent is a result of insecurity, a sense of insignificance, and shame. Competitors can be after the same goal—excellence but they cannot find it alone. The relationship among opponents should be built upon respect for each other, the game, the rules, and the honor of competition. True competition is about maintaining the honor of the opponent. We want to win and play to win, but never at the expense of the opponent's well-being. Competition is not about winning or perfection. It entails being the best you are capable of becoming based on your unique gifts, talents, and abilities. We compete with others to achieve excellence, but the person you become in the pursuit of excellence is worth far more than the apparent achievement of excellence.

Success Is about Achievements; Significance Is about Impact

Being a competitor is not dependent on your gender, your sport, or your genetics. Being a competitor is a choice, it is a decision, and it becomes a lifestyle. Competitors anticipate the great feelings that comes with succeeding by having that be their focus. They enjoy the journey as much as the result. Sometimes the fear of losing causes people to become competitive because they see losing as failure; these athletes usually find themselves competing not to lose and they sacrifice the natural joy of competing because their focus is on the final score. The ultimate competitor sees competition as an enjoyable component of life by keeping their focus on the positive aspects. They compete for an audience of one.

Too many people tend to compare their present performance with those of the past or even expectations of the future. Do not let that get in the way. Athletic performance can vary from competition to competition due to sickness, injuries, weather, rest, etc. It is our responsibility to give all of what we have at the moment. Your only comparison is with Jesus Christ. Statistics depend on game conditions. God's perspective on winning depends only upon how you perform in relation to giving all that you have

to give—leaving nothing behind, just like Jesus did on the cross.

Let's say an athlete has a personal best time 18:20 mark in a 5k race, when the athlete competes the next time and only runs a 18:56, this is failure from the world's view, but this performance can still be a victory from God's perspective. One must realize that you can still be a loser even if you statistically better your performance. How can that be? It depends entirely on how much one gives of themselves to perform as Jesus would—with the same attitude and intensity He would have.

A Christ-like athlete will never be sidetracked by the score, who the opponent is, or even the situation. A Christ-like athlete would be focused on the thought of representing Jesus, to compete to please Him in all that you say and do. As you compete in this manner, you will know with confidence that the results of the competition will be His, to bring glory and honor to Him! When this is your focus as Christ-like athlete, you become an Ultimate Competitor—an Ultimate Competitor in Christ![11]

Jesus said that anyone who wanted to follow Him had to deny Himself and take up the cross. Genuine discipleship means you go to the cross and you die. You lay it all on the altar, no matter how scary that is, because God is good and generous and will give back whatever He wants you to have. If you do not let your past die, it will not let you live. The only way to move on and have your past die is in Christ. Your identity as an ultimate competitor should be in the cross.

When this is your focus as a Christ-like athlete, you become Ultimate Competitors—Ultimate Competitors in Christ! Your performance will always follow your attitude. What approach will you take? Will you waste it? Will you resist it? Or will you invest yourself in it? God made you to be you. Significance is a choice. You need to pursue significant moments in your life while you are in them—this is what will matter. Do not try to be better than someone else or compare yourself with others; just use the gifts God has provided you to become what God wants you to become. Make each day your masterpiece.

God acts in the consistency of His character so God will continue to love you no matter where you are in your spiritual formation. God sent Jesus, His Son, because you need the power of Christ in your life to benefit from God's love and blessings. God wants to see your Christ-like character. You are never going to impress God on your own. *You need to live your life from God's smile instead of trying to live your life for His smile.*

Remember Jesus is *always* with you. He is not above you watching over you; He is not at the finish line encouraging you to finish. He walks with you in your heart. This does not make life easier—it makes it simpler. Your choices are simpler because you will apply the same set of personal standards to every situation regardless of how large or small, how private or public. There is no finish line; the finish line comes when Jesus comes back to complete us. Your race is not over until then. You can get to the finish line even though you stumble but you must make the choice to let Christ power work in your life. God loves you because of your position (His child), not because of your performance.

In order to be a champion, you need to have the foundation of values that are worthy of being a champion

GOLD PRIDE allows you an opportunity to be a person of influence on your team, the campus, and in the community. As a role model you have an impact on the sidelines, on the sidewalk as you move toward significance (faith perspective, professionally engaged, and a servant leader).

Significance is when your primary *focus* is met by achieving your objectives and the outcome of success occurs with your values intact.

"He has shown you, O man, what is good. And what does the LORD require of you? To act justly and to love mercy, and to walk humbly with your God" (Micah 6:8).

This is the Ripple Effect

One student athlete with Christian character can improve a team
One team with Christian character can improve an athletic program
One athletic program with Christian character can impact a community
From the sideline, to the sidewalk, to significance

Stat Sheet

Fundamentals: Basic Skills

1. The secret to growth in character and spiritual formation is continual evaluation and assessment. Test yourself to make sure you are solid in your faith.
    *   Review *The 7 Habits of Highly Effective People* and relate how you can apply these habits to the above statement.

Strength and Conditioning Training: Improving Your Shape

1. Character growth and your spiritual formation do not come from rules but from small actions of responsibility that occur daily. It is more important to pursue the hard right (doing the correct thing), instead of the easy wrong. When it is all said and done, your reputation does not matter. It is important, but what others think of you is simply out of yourself.
    *   What is your reputation at this time in your life?
    *   How does your reputation differ from what you think of yourself?

2. Competition can be defined as a mutual quest or striving for excellence. It is more process-oriented than outcome-oriented. Competitors strive together or with each other to bring out the best by presenting a worthy challenge. Competition, therefore, is not defined by winning and losing, but by the degree to which all competitors realize their fullest potential. Since true competition is a "mutual quest for excellence" there are no winners or losers; everyone who competes wins. This cooperative sense of competition is a value-driven process that leads to respect for others—your teammates and your opponent; personal and team integrity, being the best you are capable of becoming instead of, doing whatever it takes to get ahead and win. Your self-worth is never determined by winning or losing. Our desire to dominate an opponent is a result of insecurity, a sense of insignificance, and shame. Competitors can be after the same goal—excellence but they cannot find it alone. The relationship among opponents should be built upon respect for each other, the game, the rules, and the honor of competition. True competition is about maintaining the honor of the opponent. We want to win and play to win, but never at the expense of the opponent's well-being.

Competition is not about winning or perfection. It entails being the best you are capable of becoming based on your unique gifts, talents, and abilities. We compete with others to achieve excellence, but the person you become in the pursuit of excellence is worth far more than the apparent achievement of excellence.

- **Discuss your thoughts about what you believe competition to be and how this definition fits into your belief of competition?**

Game Day: Performing with Excellence

To become an Ultimate Competitor, you need to emulate CHRIST in competition. The acronym of CHRIST effectively describes and defines these competitive qualities.

COLLABORATION (compatibility, cooperation)
HUMILITY (competence, character)
RESILIENT (courage, creativeness)
INVESTED (competitive, commitment)
STRENGTH (complete, cognitive)
TRUTH (consistent—compassion)

On a scale of 1 to 5, with 5 being the highest value, how would you rate yourself on being an Ultimate Competitor (competing for an audience of one) at this time in your collegiate experience? Why?

Endnotes

[1] Tony Dungy. *Finding Your Path To Significance Uncommon*. Tyndale House Publishers, Inc.2009, 108.

[2] Bob Beaudine. *The Power of Who*. Center Street Hachette Book Group, 2009, 54.

[3] Tony Dungy. *Finding Your Path To Significance Uncommon*. Tyndale House Publishers, Inc.2009, 147.

[4] Tony Dungy. *Finding Your Path To Significance Uncommon*. Tyndale House Publishers, Inc.2009, 14–15.

[5] Tony Dungy. *Finding Your Path To Significance Uncommon*. Tyndale House Publishers, Inc.2009, 91.

[6] Tony Dungy. *Finding Your Path To Significance Uncommon*. Tyndale House Publishers, Inc.2009, 108.

[7] Tony Dungy. *Finding Your Path To Significance Uncommon*. Tyndale House Publishers, Inc.2009, 108–109.

[8] Tony Dungy. *Finding Your Path To Significance Uncommon*. Tyndale House Publishers, Inc.2009, 153.

[9] Tony Dungy. *Finding Your Path To Significance Uncommon*. Tyndale House Publishers, Inc.2009, 154.

[10] Jay Bilas. *Toughness Developing True Strength On and Off the Court*. New American Library: 2013, 178.

[11] "Athletic Performance Principles for Life." To The Next Level, LLC, 1999–2017. www//ttnl.org/Yrogeta.aspx?ITEMID=13

Section II

You Can Become
More Than You
Have Become

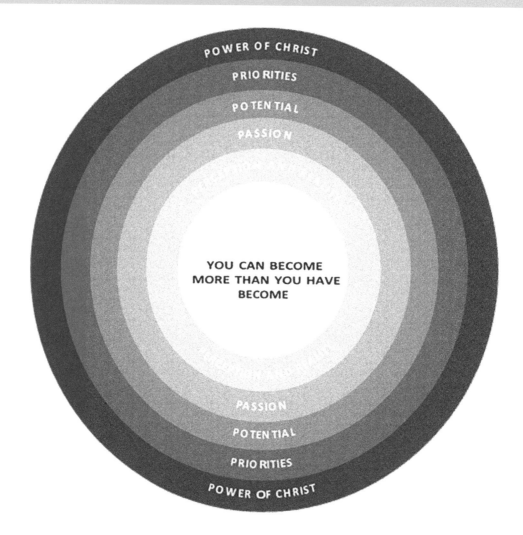

Who Am I (Sense of Self)
Whose Am I (Sense of Self in Christ)

It was a Saturday, and a young boy wanted to play with his dad. He wanted to play catch in the yard or play in the park. His dad had a different idea. The "big game" was on the television on this particular Saturday and the dad did not want to be disturbed during the game. So the dad found a picture of the world that he tore into little pieces. The dad took his son into the kitchen at the kitchen table and spread the little pieces of paper out on the table and gave the son some scotch tape. When you put the picture together, we can play. The dad thought it would take quite a while for his son to put the pieces together, thus allowing him to view the game and then they could play. To his surprise, the son returned to the living room where the television was in only a few minutes. The son had put the picture together. The dad asked, "How did you do this so fast?" This little boy looked up at his dad and said, "Before you tore the picture of the world into little pieces, I noticed a picture of a boy on the back of it. I just knew if I pasted that boy back together, the world would come together too."

The most important relationship you will ever have is with yourself. How you know and understand yourself will affect your relationship with God and others. The primary step in character development and spiritual formation is determining who you are (sense of self) and then whose you are (sense of self in Christ). When you are able to get "the picture of the boy (yourself)" together your world becomes clearer; section II is about you discovering who you are and whose you are.

Perception/Reality

He who cannot change the very fabric of his thought will never be able to change reality, and will never, therefore, make any progress.
—Anwar Sadat

Perception is the process by which people translate sensory impressions into a coherent and unified view of the world around them. Though necessarily based on incomplete and unverified or unreliable information, perception is equated with reality for most practical purposes and guides human behavior in general. Perception becomes reality. Robert White once said, "It may come as a severe shock if you have not given much thought to this subject before but our precious, cast-in-stone, objective beliefs are often totally in contrast to any reality. Or, more accurately, they are our perception of reality, rather than reality itself." An illustration of this if found in the song "Cat's in the Cradle," released by Harry Chapin in 1974; the lyrics from a poem written by his wife Sandra Gaston indicate that perception became reality. The song is about a father who is too busy to spend time with his son.

Although the song the son asks his father to join in childhood activities, the father always responds with little more than vague promises of spending time together in the future. While wishing to spend time with his father, the son starts to model himself on his father's behavior; hence, the verse in the song that says, "Wishing to be just like him." The final two verses are a reverse of the roles, where the father asks his grown-up son to visit, but the son responds that he is now too busy to find the time for his father. The father then reflects that they are both alike, saying, "My boy was just like me." This song provides perspective for the ripple effect. As a collegiate student athlete, you get caught up in the moment and lose perspective of the future. You are short-term oriented instead of long-term eternal thinking. Your mentality is that you will become more cognizant of what is important to you after your collegiate years and later in life. This is your perception, but in reality, the relationships, values, spiritual formation, and moral fiber you develop during your collegiate experience are the ones that will guide your choices later in life; therefore, making your collegiate experience paramount to your life long pursuit for excellence and significance.

The problem all college students have is the modern understanding of behavior expected from a college student or student athlete; society allows college-age students to remain childish for much longer than necessary. "Society indicates the priorities of college students and what they value are acceptance, relationships, fun, time to party, a time in their life to experience real independence that leads to the following descriptions and or perceptions: college student and drugs; college student and drinking; college student and alcohol—binge drinking; college student and sex; college student and cell phones; college student and texting; college student and social media."[1]

This holds back the development of college students from what God would like them to become because college students adhere to these perceived norms or standards and the result is low expectations. Paul in 1 Corinthians 13:11 says, "When I was a child, I spoke like a child, I thought like a child, I reasoned like a child. When I became a man/women, I gave up my childish ways." Notice Paul did not say, when I was a child, I spoke like a child, I thought like a child, I reasoned like a child. But then, I became a college student I looked like an adult, I sounded like an adult, but still acted like a child. Paul said when he became a man/women he gave up his childish ways. Paul also says in 1 Timothy 4:12, "Do not let anyone look down on you because you are young (college students), but be an example for the believers in your speech, your conduct, your love, faith, and purity."

God does not hold two standards: one for college students and one for adults. He has high expectations for both and wants both to establish high standards that model excellence. In the **GOLD PRIDE** plan the goal is to treat you like adults until you act like children.

"In 2005 Time magazine did an article on kidults; a new breed of adolescence in their mid to late twenties and beyond who offer convincing evidence that the modern concept of adolescence is not a biological stage but a cultural mind-set. What are kidults; grown men and women who still live with their parents; who dress and talk and party as they did in there collegiate years; hopping from job to job and date to date having fun but seemingly going nowhere; they neither have clear direction nor a sense of urgency. Kidults are the result of the culture myth that encourages college students to view adulthood as spoiling the fun of the collegiate experience rather than viewing it as the opportunity to invest themselves toward adhering to standards and setting expectations that will allow them to purse excellence."[2]

A difficult thing for a college student athlete to do is to go against your natural desire to fit in, to be liked, and to make friends. There is nothing quite like it for putting your convictions to the test.

"Sam Wigglesworth one of England's greatest evangelists once said, 'Great faith is the product of great fights. Great testimonies are the outcome of great tests. Great triumphs can only come out of great trials.'"[3] Three important strategies for setting higher standards and raising expectations for yourself include, (1) be known for what you do more than for what you do not do (2) to do improve your efficiency and effectiveness by performing and completing difficult tasks, and (3) pursue excellence rather than make excuses.

To live by God's standards for a college student athlete and to enjoy His blessings, you need to go beyond simply avoiding doing things that do not enhance you as an athlete or person. You need to rise above the call and be an example for others in your speech, your conduct, your love, faith, and representation. In doing difficult task, you begin to increase your level of expectation.

Identify areas where you can accomplish more by investing more of yourself. Do not be content with past accomplishments, complacency, or low expectations. Finally, pursue excellence by challenging yourself and others to call the normal things normal and save the word excellent for things that really are. Many times we fall short of our true potential because we aimed only to be bigger than the next fish in a small pond. God's standard is not for you to be the most spiritual person on your team filled with halfhearted Christians, but to "be holy" because He is holy. "God set His standards high so that we would not make the mistake of aiming low. He made them unreachable so that we would never have an excuse to stop growing."[4] Instead of just aiming to be "good" be committed to improving yourself to be all God has gifted you to be. This means establishing greater levels of excellence because there is always more that can be done. It is never a matter of arriving; it is a constant battle of growth to pursue excellence. It is that commitment to growth that kills complacency. God works through our weaknesses to accomplish His plans. "We constantly find ourselves building invisible fences; ones that keeps threats outside and us inside. We build it higher every time we say or think like: I am just not a math person; I am just not organized; my brain does not work that way; I am just not a people person. What you are really saying is that you do not want to do things that do not come easily or naturally. You do not want to break through your fears. By your actions you are also saying that God is not good and powerful enough to help you do what we cannot comfortably do on your own."[5] These actions are hard because they rest entirely on your own initiative. No one else will make you do them. However, if you do them you almost always feel good about them. "The trap is 'just do your best.' It is easy to be content with less than your best especially when our halfhearted effort seems to satisfy everyone around us. Those who could do a lot better or take a much larger challenge seldom do so when they are already good enough by other people's standards."[6] When someone says, "Just do your best are you inspired to reach more?" Or does it give you permission to just get by? Before long, you become blinded by complacency which is defined as a smug feeling of satisfaction with who you are and what you have done. Remember the enemy of great is good.

Are you content with good?

If we are willing to strive for excellence, even in boring, repetitive tasks and responsibilities that others delegate or neglect, we will reap the powerful benefits that others miss. Embracing doing things well with high expectations can make a radical difference as you navigate through your collegiate experience. Everything you do with sincere effort and the right attitude brings pleasure to God. "Whatever you do, work at it with all your heart, as working for the Lord, not for men" (Colossians 3:23).

A prayerful scripture that has helped me many times as I have reflected on the perception and reality of life and the importance of establishing a legacy is

Psalms 139:23–24
Search me, O God, and know my heart
Try me and know my anxious thoughts

And see if there is any hurtful way in me;
And lead me in the everlasting way.

The perception is there always will be time. The reality is you need to determine what is important now (WIN). What is your perception of the reality of your collegiate experience? Some people want the truth so badly, but after it has been presented to them, they deem it unacceptable. In the end, they create their own version of the truth, which is more acceptable to their perception. They deny the truth and worship the lie. It is a matter of choice for you. Are you going to stay stuck in the place you are in, or are you going to have the courage to do it and get up when you fall. This is the faith to believe in yourself; Christ can provide you the power to have faith in yourself. Realize that character development and spiritual formation is a progression (ripple effect). This is very similar to an athletic contest—a game or match has segments (halves, quarters, innings).

Just as we all sometimes struggle with our faith, so did Jesus. In times of need, we must look back and see the footprints in the sand to realize that God is, has, and always will by our side.

The Footprints Prayer

One night I had a dream . . .
I dreamed I was walking along the
beach with the Lord, and Across the
sky flashed scenes from my life.
For each scene I noticed two sets
of footprints in the sand;
One belonged to me, and
the other to the Lord.

When the last scene of my
life flashed before us,
I looked back at the footprints in the sand.
I noticed that many times
along the path of my life,

There was only one set of footprints.

I also noticed that it happened at
the very lowest and saddest
times in my life
This really bothered me, and I
questioned the Lord about it.
"Lord, you said that once I
decided to follow you,
You would walk with me all the way;
But I have noticed that during the
most troublesome times in my life,
There is only one set of footprints.
I don't understand why in times
when I needed you the most, you
should leave me."

The Lord replied, "My
precious, precious child.
I love you, and I would never,
never leave you during your times
of trial and suffering. When you
saw only one set of footprints,
It was then that I carried you."

What defines you? How can you live life as if Jesus were you or how would Jesus live your life? At no other time in your life are you better positioned to decide who you will become; you have strength, sharp minds, and energetic bodies. In order to accomplish things and move toward significance, you have to care more about pleasing God than you do about pleasing the people around you. *Jesus is the light of the world but He needs to become the light of your world. The Ripple Effect to Character Development and Spiritual Formation* provides you with a perspective to know who you are, whose you are, as well as an understanding of the concept of **GOLD PRIDE**. Implementing the "rules of the road" provides you a foundation to build your collegiate experience to become more than you have become to be a role model, a mentor leader, and the ultimate competitor.

Ephesians 4:22–24

"But that's no life for you. You learned Christ! My assumption is that you have paid careful attention to Him, been well instructed in the truth precisely as we have it in Jesus. Since, then, we do not have the excuse of ignorance, everything—and I do mean everything— connected with that old way of life has to go. It's rotten through and through. Get rid of it! And then take on an entirely new way of life—a God-fashioned life, a life renewed from the inside and working itself into your conduct as God accurately reproduces His character in you."

Perception

The perception is there always will be time.

Stat Sheet

Fundamentals: Basic Skills

1. Discuss the phase "The perception is there always will be time." What does this mean to you at this time as you begin your collegiate experience?

Strength and Conditioning Training: Improving Your Shape

Is the statement below perception or reality? Why has this image been created? Could people perceive you in this manner, why or why not?

The problem all college students have is the modern understanding of behavior expected from a college student or student athlete; society allows college-age students to remain childish for much longer than necessary. "Society indicates the priorities of college students and what they value are acceptance, relationships, fun, time to party, a time in their life to experience real independence that leads to the following descriptions and or perceptions: college student and drugs; college student and drinking; college student and alcohol—binge drinking; college student and sex; college student and cell phones; college student and texting; college student and social media."

Game Day: Performing with Excellence

1. A difficult thing for a college student athlete to do is to go against your natural desire to fit in, to be liked, and to make friends. There

is nothing quite like it for putting your convictions to the test.

Important strategies for setting higher standards and raising expectations for yourself include the following"

(1) Be known for what you do more than for what you do not do.
(2) To do improve your efficiency and effectiveness by performing and completing difficult tasks.

(3) Pursue excellence rather than make excuses.

How can you apply these strategies into your collegiate experience?

Endnotes

1   Alex and Brett Harris. *Do Hard Things*. Multnomah Books: 2008, 37.
2   Alex and Brett Harris. *Do Hard Things*. Multnomah Books: 2008, 50–51.
3   Alex and Brett Harris. *Do Hard Things*. Multnomah Books: 2008, 71.
4   Alex and Brett Harris. *Do Hard Things*. Multnomah Books: 2008, 101.
5   Alex and Brett Harris. *Do Hard Things*. Multnomah Books: 2008, 71.
6   Alex and Brett Harris. *Do Hard Things*. Multnomah Books: 2008, 88.

Passion

Passion helps you identify your destination

Mike Krzyzewski, men's basketball coach at Duke University and the USA Olympic Team, has won more games than any other NCAA Men's Division I basketball coach and has won four NCAA Basketball Championships related this story in his book, *Leading With The Heart*:

While I sat out the season, our team fell apart and we finished with a 13–18 record. So upon my return, I had to build the program back up again—hopefully, to where it had once been. In order to do that, I had to accept the fact that the team had deteriorated because I had allowed us to get away from our core. Heck, I had actually deteriorated physically because I got away from my own core.

Sometimes in our haste to accomplish, we forget why we are doing it. The truth is that I had violated the basic premises that originally allowed us to achieve all our success. Now I had to get back to them.

I pulled out a videotape of Quin Snyder's senior speech and I wrote down those words he mentioned: commitment, integrity, toughness, honesty, collective responsibility, pride, love, and friendship. I placed the list in my notebook and carried it around with me. And I vowed to myself that we, as a team, would get back to the core principles on that list—because that is what made us go. It certainly is what made me go. Getting back to those things would then lead to winning the ACC regular season, winning the tournament, going to the Big Dance, going to the Final Four.

I also thought back to the earlier days of my coaching career—even all the way back to when I was a kid in Chicago. I remembered that we did not have organized leagues, that we did not get trophies for winning. We just played the game.

We played because we enjoyed it. We played because we were friends. We played for innocence.[1]

Your heart reveals the real you. The heart is not just an organ but the center of who you are. Another word for heart is passion. Each person needs to determine and articulate their passion. What does a person love to do? Passion determines why you say the things you do or why you feel the way you do. Passion is why you act the way you do. It is what you truly are, not what others think you are or what they think you should be or what circumstances force you to be. The Bible uses the term heart to describe the bundle of desire, hopes, interests, ambitions, dreams, and affections you have. Your heart represents the source of all your motivations and what you care about most. "As a face reflected in water, so the heart reflects the person" (Proverbs 27:19).

If you are passionate about something, you do it because you love the joy of the participation and not the attention you may derive from the participation. This is really true for the passionate student athlete. We all have a unique emotional heartbeat that establishes what we think about subjects, activities, or circumstances that interest us. The experiences that excite you reveal the nature of your *heart*—your *passion*. This love allows you to put your heart in it every day. "Serve the Lord with all your heart" (Ephesians 6:6).

Do not ignore the interest of your *heart*. Consider how these interests might be used for God's glory. There is a reason you love to do the things you do. Serving God from your *heart* allows for increased *effectiveness*. *Passion* drives perfection. If you do not care about a task, it is unlikely that you will excel at it. The highest achievers in any field are those who do it because of *passion*, not duty or profit.

"It has been said that the great men and women of history were great not for what they owned or earned, but for what they gave their lives to accomplish."[2] President Woodrow Wilson, former US president, once said, "We grow by dreams (pursuing our passion). All big [individuals] are dreamers. They see things in soft haze of a spring day or in the red fire on a long winter's evening. Some of us let those dreams die, but others nourish and protect them; nourish them through bad days until they bring them to the sunshine and light which comes always to those who sincerely hope that their dreams will come true. Passion is the fuel that helps people nourish and protect their dreams."[3]

Our goal is to help each student athlete experience the joy of participation, to be able to compete with excellence and belong as a person not just an athlete. We want to facilitate the process to help each student athlete connect their heart to maximize their passion.

"If only you would **prepare your heart** and lift up your hands to Him in prayer! **Get rid of your sins and leave all iniquity behind you.** Then your face will brighten in innocence. You'll be strong and free of fear. You will forget your misery. It will be gone like water under the bridge" (Job 11:13–16).

"**Whatever you do**, whether in word or deed, do it all in the name of the Lord Jesus, giving thanks to God the Father through Him" (Colossians 3:17).

This is God's definition of passion. Most of us have just enough God to bug us not to bless us—this is casual Christianity. God gives His best to those who want it the most. Where is your passion?

Perception

The perception is there always will be time.

Passion

Passion is the fuel that helps people nourish and protect their dreams.

Stat Sheet

Fundamentals: Basic Skills

1. What is passion?

Strength and Conditioning Training: Improving Your Shape

1. "One person with a PASSION is equal to 100 with interest."
   - _____ is an integral part of your life.
   - **Write your sport in blank.**
   - Every season is a journey. Every journey is a lifetime.
   - During the season, your team should be led with exuberance and excitement.
   - You should live the journey—live it right, live it together, live it shared.
   - You should try to make one another better.
   - You should get on one another if somebody's not doing their part.
   - You should hug one another when they are.
   - You should be disappointed in a loss and exhilarated in a win—it is all about the journey.
   - It should be honest and it should be real.
   - It is not about winning games or what other people's expectations of us may be.
   - Play for innocence (for the love of the game, *passion*).

2. What does it mean to you to play your sport with passion for the innocence of the game?

Game Day: Performing with Excellence

1. Frank Irving Fletcher once observed, "No man can deliver the goods if his heart is heavier than his load." There is a difference between things that touch your heart and things that weight you down.
   - In pursuing your passion, what are the things that bring you joy?

How does your relationship with Christ nourish your passion?

Endnotes

[1] Mike Krzyzewski. *Leading With the Heart*. Warner Books: 2001, 272–273.

[2] James Maxwell, *Becoming a Person of Influence*. Nashville: Thomas Nelson, 1997, 145–146.

[3] James Maxwell. *Becoming a Person of Influence*. Nashville: Thomas Nelson, 1997, 132.

Potential

I am only one, but I am one. I cannot do everything, but I can do something. And I will not let what I cannot do interfere with what I can do. And by the grace of God, I will.
—Edward Everett Hale

Psychologist Sheldon Kopp once stated, "All significant battles are waged within the self."[1] Potential is wrapped up in the gifts and talents God gave you. It is the ability, skills, knowledge, and desire you have to achieve and perform.

Potential is defined as "the inherent ability or capacity for growth, development, or coming into being." John Maxwell in his book, *Becoming a Person of Influence*, states, "There is not a person in the world who does not have the desire to be someone, to have significance." In discussing or determining one's potential this statement is extremely relative. "We all have the potential to be someone but we all do not succeed in attaining our true potential."[2]

Unrealized potential is a tragic waste. Composer Gian Carlo Menotti once stated, "Hell begins on that day when God grants us a clear vision of all that we might have achieved, of all the gifts we wasted, of all that we might have done that we did not do."[3] The challenge in determining and reaching your potential is between what you have done and what you are capable of doing. This is especially true of collegiate student athletes. Most of you come to the next level (college) with credentials that indicate you can become a quality athlete. However, you find yourselves in a dilemma because

you face new challenges in competition, in the classroom and in your relationships. In most cases, the dilemma is not about your skill level in athletics; you have faced these challenges before and have overcome them. For most, it is a lack of values or principles to face the adversity and be able to move forward. This then becomes an attitude or character problem.

Maxwell states, "Character is like a tree and reputation like its shadow. The shadow is what we think of it; the tree is the real thing. The ultimate measure of a man or woman is not where they stand in moments of comfort or convenience, but where they stand at times of challenge and controversy."[4]

When you were a child you were full of creative ideas, they never stopped flowing because you had an open mind and belief in yourself that you could do anything. In fact you most likely drove your parent's crazy with all your ideas and dreams. As you grow up the fear of acceptance, peer pressure, conforming to societal norms, become more important than the development of yourself to your true potential. Conforming is more important than development because of this you are held back from what you could do, for what God made you to do and even from what you want to do. You develop yourself with low expectation instead of developing high expectations for yourself and your potential.

"Most people are funny; they want to get ahead and succeed, but they are reluctant to change. They are often willing to grow only enough to accommodate their problems; instead they need to grow enough to achieve their potential"[5] The essence of potential is not determined by what you do but who you are. The development of values and principles that guide your choices and decisions in life lead you toward significance and success. You have the potential to make a difference with your life if you can discover these things about yourself (the criteria for becoming an Ultimate Competitor):

1. **Identity**: Who you are.
2. **Integrity**: You have standards that establish what you stand for.
3. **Intimacy**: You understand who cares about you and who you care about—are you a great teammate.
4. **Interdependence**: You understand that your platform will influence others as a role model.
5. **Industry (destiny)**: What you can do with your life—you are capable to provide mentoring for those that come after you.

Many years ago, I came across this slogan that really defines *potential*:

Be what you is;
Because if you be what you
ain't You ain't what you is

There are many components to your potential that need to be met for you to achieve your true potential. Each component has a ripple effect on the other in determining your success to achieve. These components include a balance between your social, physical, emotional, intellectual, and spiritual potential. Many times especially in a student athlete's life when the term *potential* is used it assumed that the only component one is talking about is physical poten-

tial. However, if you are going to "be what you is" to move toward and reach significance there needs to be emphasis on all the components of potential.

To develop the components of your potential you need to be intentional and honest with yourself recognizing your strengths and weakness and what components need to be improved upon to achieve balance. To achieve balance, you need others to have faith and believe in you, to provide support, guidance, and encouragement. The person that believes in you establishes a quality relationship with you, cares about you, will allow your self-worth to be strengthened. You need to feel good about yourself for the components of potential to develop. It is difficult, if not almost impossible, to achieve your potential on your own, through a connection with others, faith, and hope are established. Hope is perhaps one of the greatest gifts one can provide for another because if your sense of self is weak you will fail to see your own potential and significance; hope gives you a reason to keep trying and striving to reach your potential in the future. A person can live forty days without food, four days without water, four minutes without air, but only four seconds without hope. A sense of security is important to reach potential. People are reluctant to trust and reach their potential when they do not feel secure. "When people are made to feel secure and important and appreciated, it will no longer be necessary for them to whittle down others in order to seem bigger in comparison."[6]

"For most people it is not what they are that holds them back. It is what they think they are not."[7] Most people do not have faith in themselves. They believe that they will fail or not measure up to others expectations. They see difficulty in everything they do. However, the reality is that difficulties seldom defeat us; your lack of faith does. Today in our culture, most people do not have a sense of community, they feel isolated. They have lived in a society that has continually torn them down rather than believing in them. We all need to have someone in our lives that has faith in us so we can have faith in ourselves. W. T. Purkiser, said this, "Faith is more than thinking something is true. Faith is thinking something is true to the extent that we act on it."[8] Others can stop you temporarily, but you are the only one who can do it permanently.

Through *The Ripple Effect* you need to clearly define your purpose. Purpose provides a unique source of passion and perseverance and a path to follow. When you do not know where you are going, any road will do. Our heart is where we must look to find the answer to why we do what we do in life, our purpose for being. If your purpose is centered on selfish gains like wealth or power, or success, or even centered on the fear of losing, then you will be failing to live up to your true potential. But if the purpose of your heart is focused on a relationship with Christ, then you can truly become the best you were created to be.

In the book *Do Hard Things,* the author used the example of a diving board to provide you with an illustration of perspective of most college-age students:

"Diving boards have a sweet spot. If you take a big leap and land just right the board will launch you up into the air and down into the pool in a perfect swan dive. If you miss the sweet spot things do not work out as well. Your body jolts, the board clunks, and you bounce, teeter, and career into the water maybe even doing a belly flop. The symbolism here is as follows:

1. The pool is your future life.
2. The diving board is your present life.
3. The myth of what society sees as the behavior and conduct of a college student is that it is time to party beside the pool but the fact is you are already on the diving board.

The whole purpose of the diving board is to launch you, with purpose and precision, into your future. You will either make a successful dive into adulthood or deliver something closer to a belly flop if you fail to launch during your collegiate years. Are you standing at the end of the diving board but will not jump because you waited too long to launch; choosing a direction or purpose, developing character, and building momentum for significance."[9]

James Baldwin said, "In order to become an effective teammate it is important to take a look inside yourself." Identify what drives and motivates you, the areas in which you are naturally gifted, and the areas that are more challenging. A personal inventory can help you to understand and evaluate the things that make you tick. What makes you think, react, and respond the way you do and what makes you to the things you do. The ability to do this is sign of maturity. Questions to ask yourself: how do others around me flourish as a result of my choices? How does my leadership involvement in their lives in whatever setting we are in have a positive and lasting influence and impact on them?

Remember

Success is about achievements; significance is about impact.

The hope is that as you develop a better understanding of who you are, that God made you for a purpose and how you can use your gifts and talents to honor God and that you take ownership of your life choices. This requires making choices based on a foundational principle. There is no growth without change, no change without loss, and with loss comes pain. Life is about choices; you cannot have it all, you need to sacrifice something.

Only when you have a sense of peace about yourself and who you are will you be able to purse your potential in earnest. "No factor is more decisive in people's psychological development and motivation than the value judgments they make about themselves. The nature of self-evaluation has a profound effect on a person's values, beliefs, thinking process, feelings, needs, and goals. Self-esteem is the most significant key to a person's behavior."[10]

The top three sources of insecurity are **rejection**, love being withheld and your input or opinions do not matter; **criticism**, you can never please or measure up; **comparison**, this might be the worst because it influences what is important, what is success and how we ought to think.

The security necessary to overcome self-doubt and obtain the kind of confidence in yourself that is not shaken by circumstances is best obtained through a relationship with God. To be secure, trustworthy, and loyal to yourself and others you need to be authentic. Others will know when you are not. In times of crisis, people will look at your character, not your competence or authority but your character.

Ephesians 1:4–5 says, "Even before the world was made, God had already chosen us to be His through our union with Christ, so that we would be holy and without fault before Him. If you surrender to what God wants you to do you can develop your true potential and live your dream."

Dreams exist in your heart. This is the claim stated in Ephesians 1:4–5. God gave you a dream before you were born, and you finally woke up to it. Your dream is to do what you do best and what you most love to do. Why have you missed this for so long? You will have to sacrifice and make some changes to pursue your dream. But it will be worth it.

Your dream will take you out of your current comfort zone. Dreams pull on you. Reality will hit and you will hit the wall of fear. You need to stop being afraid of being afraid. You must move out of comfort zone and overcome fear. This takes courage; your dream is on the other side of the wall of fear. It is difficult to leave comfort zone, but it would be harder to leave behind your dream. When you move to the edge of your comfort zone, it will affect others comfort zone. Every dream has risks, or it will not happen. People or circumstances or situation will attempt to hold you back. There will be some people that you have never met that will attempt to derail you and your dream. When you leave your comfort zone, it will upset some of those close to you. If you cannot persuade these people to *believe* in you, in the end you need to decide whom you would please. If you are going to pursue the dream, you need to please the dream maker, you.

In developing your potential it is important to **BELIEVE**:

BELIEVE you are capable of becoming more than you have become. You need to have faith that you can reach your potential.

EMPHASIZE character development and skill strength. Sharpen skills that already exist. Learning to conduct yourself with integrity in every situation and circumstance will enhance your ability to reach your potential.

LIST your past successes. This provides encouragement that you can get to the next level.

INCLUDE others in your journey. We are better together. Belonging is one of the most important and basic human needs. Everyone needs somebody to come alongside them—to help them, to hold them accountable. If you understand this process and are willing to become vulnerable to include others in your journey and allow them to help you, their lives will be changed as well as yours. Albert LaLonde says, "Many young people today have never experienced a deep emotional attachment to anyone. They do not know how to love and be loved. The need to be loved translates itself into the need to belong to someone or something."

EXERCISE positive attitude. James Maxwell defines attitude in his book, *The Winning Attitude* as "Attitude is an inward feeling expressed by behavior." Your attitude toward self-improvement is the primary force that will determine whether you will succeed or fail. "The future not only looks bright when the attitude is right, but also the present is much more enjoyable. The positive person understands that the journey is as enjoyable as the destination."[11]

VISUALIZE your development. Begin with the end in mind. Try to understand what you are capable of becoming. Approach your potential with enthusiasm. Attempt to visualize obstacles to your development, things that might be a distraction, what really matters to you, what makes you tick and see yourself becoming who you want to become.

EXPECT excellence. According to Dennis Waitley, "The winner's edge is not in a gifted birth, a high IQ, or in talent. The winner's edge is all in the attitude not aptitude." Attitude is the criterion for success. As people's attitudes change from doubt to confidence in themselves and their ability to succeed and their potential—everything in their lives changes for the better."[12] Become competent in the three *E*s, empathy, excellence, and emulating Christ.

Every person has the potential to make a difference. Are you willing to accept this challenge for your life? You can make a difference by developing your potential by using the gifts and talents God gave you for His glory. "In life, the price tag that the world puts on us is almost identical to the one we put on ourselves. People who have a great deal of self-respect and who believe that they are significant are usually respected and made to feel valued by others."[13]

Perception

The perception is there always will be time.

Passion

Passion is the fuel that helps people nourish and protect their dreams.

Potential

The challenge in determining and reaching your potential is between what you have done and what you are capable of doing.

Stat Sheet

Fundamentals: Basic Skills

1. What is potential?
2. Diving boards have a sweet spot. If you take a big leap and land just right the board will launch you up into the air and down into the pool in a perfect swan dive. If you miss the sweet spot things do not work out as well. Your body jolts, the board clunks, and you bounce, teeter, and career into the water maybe even doing a belly flop. The symbolism here is as follows:
   - The pool is your future life.
   - The diving board is your present life.
   - The myth of what society sees as the behavior and conduct of a college student is that it is time to party beside the pool but the fact is you are already on the diving board.

The whole purpose of the diving board is to launch you, with purpose and precision, into your future. You will either make a successful dive into adulthood or deliver something closer to a belly flop if you fail to launch during your collegiate years. Are you standing at the end of the diving board but will not jump because you waited too long to launch, choosing a direction or purpose, developing character, and building momentum for significance.

3. Are you on the diving board or beside the pool?

Strength and Conditioning Training: Improving Your Shape

1. Rick Warren's book, *What on Earth Am I Here For*, is entitled "You Are Not an Accident." If God made you for a purpose, why do we limit your potential with self-imposed limitation?
2. These *statements* tend to limit potential:

- It has never been done before
- I cannot do that
- I will never try that again
- **Make a list of things that have limited your potential.**

3. In defining your potential you need to keep this concept in mind, you will never move further than the boundaries of self-imposed limitations.

TRAINED FLEAS AND LIMITATIONS

Have you ever visited a carnival and watched a flea circus? These tiny insects make tremendous leaps, yet never go beyond a predetermined height. Each flea seems to recognize an invisible ceiling. Why? Because the fleas are trained under a transparent glass dome; even when the dome is removed, they still observe its limitations.

Unfortunately, many people are like these trained fleas. Since they were placed under hindering circumstances early in life, they formed the habit of self-limitation. As college students, they do not use their untapped potential.

Do not let this happen to you. Change your self-concept – raise your sights – expand your horizons and *shatter the ceiling of your restrictions*.

LIMITATIONS OF AN ALARM CLOCK

An alarm clock can wake you up,
But you have to get yourself out of bed.
A teacher can warn you will fail,
But to pass you must start using our head.
A stumble serves notice you have been careless But you must then step lively, or you will fall. A coach can show you how to keep from traveling, But, to score it is you who must shoot the ball. There may be signals to guide and direct,
But it is up to you to steer
through traffic's flow;
In life the world will pose crucial questions,
But the answers you must learn to know

- What does Romans 12:3 mean to you in helping you achieve the components of your potential?

"I'm speaking to you out of deep gratitude for all that God has given me, and especially as I have responsibilities in relation to you. Living then, as every one of you does, in pure grace, it's important that you not misinterpret yourselves as people who are bringing this goodness to God. No, God brings it all to you. The only accurate way to understand ourselves is by what God is and by what he does for us, not by what we are and what we do for him."

Game Day: Performing with Excellence

1. You have the potential to make a difference in your life if you can discover these things about your-

self. Take time now to write out where you are in each area in your life today.

- **Identity:** Who you are
- **Integrity:** You have standards that establish what you stand for.
- **Intimacy:** You understand who cares about you and who care about-are you a great teammate.
- **Interdependence:** You understand that your platform will influence others as a role model.
- **Industry (destiny)**: What you can do with your life-you are capable to provide mentoring for those that come after you.

Endnotes

1   James Maxwell. *Becoming a Person of Influence.* Nashville: Thomas Nelson, 1997, 204.
2   James Maxwell. *Becoming a Person of Influence.* Nashville: Thomas Nelson, 1997, 105.
3   James Maxwell. *Becoming a Person of Influence.* Nashville: Thomas Nelson, 1997, 130.
4   James Maxwell. *Becoming a Person of Influence.* Nashville: Thomas Nelson, 1997, 132.
5   James Maxwell. *Becoming a Person of Influence.* Nashville: Thomas Nelson, 1997, 126.
6   James Maxwell. *Becoming a Person of Influence.* Nashville: Thomas Nelson, 1997, 43.
7   James Maxwell. *Becoming a Person of Influence.* Nashville: Thomas Nelson, 1997, 52.
8   James Maxwell. *Becoming a Person of Influence.* Nashville: Thomas Nelson, 1997, 65.
9   Alex and Brett Harris. *Do Hard Things.*(Multnomah Books: 2008, 48–49.
10 James Maxwell. *Becoming a Person of Influence.* Nashville: Thomas Nelson, 1997, 49.
11 James Maxwell. *The Winning Attitude.* Nashville: Thomas Nelson, 1997, 43.
12 James Maxwell. *Becoming a Person of Influence.* Nashville: Thomas Nelson, 1997, 72.
13 James Maxwell. *Becoming a Person of Influence.* Nashville: Thomas Nelson, 1997, 53.

Priorities

Things that matter most must never be at the mercy of things which matter least.
—Goethe

Priorities align what is important to you, your passion. As you assign priorities to all the important elements in your life, you will begin to demonstrate your true passion and what is really important to you by what you choose to do first, second, third, and so on. Aligning your priorities in accordance with your passion and potential will assist you in establishing your purpose that is necessary if you want to achieve excellence. If you are not directing your life, making decision for your destiny, you are allowing yourself to drift through life.

By aligning your priorities with your passion, the desire is that your ability to perform in all areas of your life will be more consistent, allowing you to reach significance. Without clear and concise priorities, you keep changing directions. You may say that something is important to you, but in the end, your actions will determine if you are serious about it. Using your platform as a student athlete to influence and guide teammates, provides a barometer to measure your influence through the consistency of your actions and words. This is what you believe; therefore, this is what you will see.

As a student athlete, your responsibility and focus is to pursue excellence toward significance. "The power of focusing can be seen in light. Diffused light has little power or impact, but you can concentrate its energy by focusing it. With a magnifying glass, the rays of the sun can be focused to set grass or paper on fire. When light is focused even more as a laser beam, it can cut through steel."[1] Significance is the management by objectives; it looks beyond the focus on outcomes (scoreboard) to a leadership model that is actually management by values as well as objectives and outcomes. True significance comes when you reach those objectives and outcomes with your values still intact. In achieving significance you put your personal signature on everything you do. Significance is all about impact.

Significance fosters this thought process. What does God want you to become? This is a higher purpose. The very nature of God is to have goodness in so much abundance that it overflows into our lives. Make it a lifelong commitment to ask God every day to bless you and while you are at it to bless you a lot. God's bounty is limited only by us, not by His resources, power, or willingness to give.

The true path of significant performance comes as a result of stability and success. Success is building value in you. Significance is creating value in and for others. While you desire to have significant performance, you need a foundation of values or principles to provide security and sustainability for these performances, significance is unsustainable without stability.

Discipline provides stability in one's life. Discipline is a tool to establish principles, values, or standards that modify behavior. Discipline comes from the derivative disciple. The word disciple has biblical connotations because the twelve followers of Christ were called disciples. If you are disciplined person your discipline comes from within. You are a disciple, a follower of your own principles and values that are guided by your spiritual formation. Discipline is paramount in establishing priorities.

Discipline is a positive quality for a student athlete. There are four important disciplines:

1. Discipline of *honesty*
2. Discipline of *self*
3. Discipline to *respect authority*
4. Discipline of *habit*

Discipline of Honesty

You need to develop the discipline to tell the truth. The truth needs to be the basis for all you do. Through the truth trusting relationship are developed. The choice for the discipline of honesty enhances relationships and helps build the team concept because each team member knows that each of their teammates embrace the personal responsibility to develop themselves toward significance. Everyone is working to not let their teammates down. This leads to a greater respect in the each relationship and teammate so the game can be played with passion.

Discipline of Self

This is the responsibility and accountability component of discipline. It is your ability as an individual to establish trustworthiness with yourself as well as your teammates and coaches. Trustworthiness of self is the ability to trust yourself to be responsible and accountable. Trustworthiness for team, can your teammates count on you.

The choice to discipline self, embraces personal responsibility and accountability; you become more consistent and reliable in every situation because you have developed more self-control as well as being more focused because you are implementing your principles and values.

Discipline to Respect Authority

This is your willingness to establish a belief in a higher authority.

The story of Moses reflects the discipline to respect authority.

Moses regarded disgrace for the sake of Christ as a greater value than the treasures of Egypt because he was looking ahead to his reward (long-term gain). Moses established his priorities forsaking being the son of Pharaoh's daughter. He needed to decide if he would return to be a slave or remain an Egyptian royalty. He realized God made him for a purpose and that was to be used by God to lead the Israelites out of bondage. Moses refused to live a lie; are you living a lie trying to be someone you are not?

God made you to be you. Moses needed to decide who he was.

Your spiritual formation in establishing priorities is dependent on your relationship with a higher authority. Moses told Pharaoh that he reported to a higher power.

As a student athlete, you must have the discipline to believe and trust in what the leader, the person in authority, has to say and many times in a moment's notice. If an athlete or a team cannot perform with excellence at a moment's notice they probably have not developed the discipline to respect authority. This trigger is called instant belief. Instant belief is developed over time through the building of trust between you and the person in authority. The person in authority accentuates the development of instant belief by being direct and communicating regularly with integrity through honest communication, validating that their word is good. In the long run, most people will respect and appreciate someone who is honest with them. Romans 6:16–19 (MSG) says, "Hardly. You know well enough from your own experience that there are some acts of so-called freedom that destroy freedom. Offer yourselves to sin, for instance, and it's your last free act. But offer yourselves to the ways of God and the freedom never quits. All your lives you've let sin tell you what to do. But thank God you've started listening to a new master, one whose commands set you free to live openly in His freedom! I'm using this freedom language because it's easy to picture. You can readily recall, can't you, how at one time the more you did just what you felt like doing—not caring about others, not caring about God—the worse your life became and the less freedom you had? And how much different is it now as you live in God's freedom, your lives healed and expansive in holiness?" When you begin to put first things first in establishing your priorities and the discipline to respect authority remember to include your relationship with Christ.

Discipline of Habit

Habits need to be formed by design. You must develop and have guiding principles to form quality habits. The habits you develop will reflect what you will compromise and what you will not compromise. Will your actions meet your principle or values or will you adjust your principles or values to meet your actions? You cannot live off spiritual commitment of others (parents, friends, etc.). You need to make our own spiritual commitment and develop your own faith. "Our purpose is to please God, not people. He is the one who examines the motives of our hearts" (Thessalonians 2:4). "Do not follow the crowd in doing wrong" (Exodus 23:2).

Moses chose to be mistreated along with the people of God rather than enjoy the pleasures of sin for a short time. Most of the problems in your life will be your inability to delay gratification. We live in a culture today that promotes comfort, not challenges. We want for things now, instant gratification, free from the consequences of our choices and easy as possible. Moses first needed to refuse Pharaoh then he chose the people. Many times you need to break an old habit before you can build a new habit.

You are a product of your past but not a prisoner of your past. You have the power to choose a better life by developing Christ-like habits. This is what Moses did, "We can have joy in our troubles, because we know that these troubles produce patience. And patience produces character, and character produces hope" (Romans 5:3–4). To develop Christ-like habits you need to learn how to do the tough things earlier in life. For a disciplined person your discipline comes from within. The right thing to do is usually the hard thing to do.

Priorities are the values that drive your life and define your spiritual essence. We all talk about our priorities in life. We can list them without a second thought. But sometimes our list of priorities falls into the same wastepaper basket as our New Year's resolutions. We talk about them, but that's as far as it gets. Our task is to put our life priorities into action. To do this your priorities need to include the following:

1. They need to be principle and value-centered. This allows you to use your time on what is really important and effective for your purpose. Everything is not really, really important.
2. They need to have balance. This identifies the various constituents that you need to support. There is not enough time to do everything.
3. They need to have a spiritual context. Many times in our busyness we tend to give God our leftovers.

Establishing priorities with these three criteria allows you to establish your priorities in harmony with your deepest values, defining your short-term and long-term objectives that include your spiritual formation. The way you spend your time tells a lot about your real priorities. If your list of priorities does not resemble what matters most in your daily activities, decide if you really want to live out your chosen priorities or if you just want to keep telling yourself that these priorities are important to you. Talk is cheap.

How Do I Discover My Identity: What Defines You

Who are you letting define your identity? If you live for the approval of others, you die by their criticism. You need to make our own spiritual commitment and develop your own faith. People can hurt or scar you but no one can ruin your life but you.

What makes you, you? It is a combination of factors. You need to look at all the dimensions of your life. "A person who fears God deals responsibly with all of reality not just a piece of it" (Ecclesiastes 7:18). Everything in your life is unique and unique to you. God will not evaluate you on talent you do not have but on what you did with the gifts and talents you were given. Remember, you had no control over what was given to you, your talent.

Five factors that influence your identity; what your gifts and talents are the following:

1. Chemistry (DNA): biology, your body
2. Connections: your relationships
3. Circumstances: Situations that make you, you, things around you that affect your life.
4. Consciousness: How you talk to yourself
5. Choices: Man is made in the image of God, man can make a moral choice

As you begin to develop what defines you, you want to look in the mirror to develop an honest assessment of yourself currently and develop a vision for your collegiate experience that will allow you to move toward significance in your lifetime. **You can become more than you have become.**

"For I know the plans I have for you" declares the Lord, Plans to prosper you and not to harm you, plans to give you hope and a future . . ." (Jeremiah 29:11).

You should never put blinders on and overlook your personal development and life issues. You need to examine and identify any problems you might have in your life. If you do not go through this process you will tend to self-meditate on your insecurities, doubts, pain, and problems. Therefore, you tend to believe you do not measure up to societal expectations and you look for other means to satisfy your sense of being, which include alcohol, drugs, sex, pornography, and a host of other stimulates or meds.

One of the goals of *The Ripple Effect* is to help with this process by a means of being honest with you so you can be honest with yourself and others. It requires building a trust and heartfelt care that allows you to make sense of who you are and help you to find your identity and God's purpose for your gifts and talents.

Belonging is especially critical to a collegiate athlete in developing their sense of identity and self-worth. To be a part of a whole greater than one's self is critical to a student athlete's well-being and self-discovery. Every person has specific gifts, talents, and life experiences that direct them toward specific purposes and routes in life. Every person in the journey of self-discovery needs to face their self-doubts, insecurities, and life experiences that seem easier

to repress than process. To become a better person and find your identity a person needs to fully understand their feelings and emotions that determine the way they act. One must review and critique the culture in which they live and the confusing messages they receive from movies, music, magazines, media, and what is societal image of what a collegiate athlete should be. You need to liberate yourselves from these false messages and become the person you believe yourself to be. Each person needs to act in accordance with their God given potential and value and move away from the cultural biases that exist in our society. Personal reflection lays the foundation for relational, athletic, ethical excellence.

The challenge for you is to examine your identity, define your priorities and the impact this identity has on your development, your teammates, your family, your relationships, and the community. You find your identity in what God says about you. Only God knows your full potential. Most people live for the expectations of others. If you are always trying to meet someone else's purpose for your life you will miss God's purpose for your life. An important part of your collegiate experience is to begin to understand your identity in Christ. What *purpose* does Christ have for your life and how you can live out those expectations? Walt Disney said, "Think beyond your lifetime if you want to establish something worthwhile."

We let cultural expectations become our standard, we allow ourselves to be squeezed into a mold, with little room for Christ like character and competence. We live in a culture that wants to tell us how to act, how to think, how to look, and how to talk. It wants to tell us what to wear, what to buy, and where to buy it. It wants to tell us what to dream, what to value, and what to live for. Where expectations are high we tend to rise to meet them. Where expectations are low we tend to drop to meet them.

Culture says character is connected to external validation:

1. Appearances: how you look, what you do, your activities (if you are busy and involved you will be accepted).
2. Attachments: Who you are associated with allows you to become the right person.
3. Conquer: What you conquer or possess you become (your cars, clothes, relationships).
4. Conform: You watch the popular ones and see what it takes to be accepted and then make the adjustments in your lifestyle and actions to fit in. You become part of the group by emulation instead of being who you are (developing yourself).
5. Command: To be in charge of something or in control of something or someone.

The college experience is not a vacation from responsibility; it is a training ground of future leaders who dare to be responsible now. You do not need others approval to be happy. Happiness is a choice. Jesus said, "Your approval or disapproval means nothing to me" (John 5:41). Someone's disap-

proval does not mean you cannot be happy. "I am the one who comforts you! So why are you afraid of mere humans, who wither like the grass and disappear?" (Isaiah 51:12). Jesus sets you free from the expectations of others. If you are looking for someone else for needs or happiness you will be let down.

What seems so important now is only temporal. Think about what was important to you in middle school; is it important to you now? You need to focus on long-term investments not short-term pleasures. Your collegiate experience should be about pursuing what is important to you now basing your choices on long-term thinking. "The world and everything in it that people desire is passing away; but those who do the will of God will live forever" (1 John 2:17). Jesus said, "The things that are highly valued by people are worth nothing in God's sight" (Luke 16:15b).

As an Ultimate Competitor, you only have to please one person, an audience of one. Jesus said, "I do not try to please myself, but I only please the One who sent me" (John 5:30). This does not make life easier it makes simpler. Paul said, "I am not trying to be a people pleaser! No I am trying to please God. If I were still trying to please people, I would not be Christ's servant" (Galatians 1:10).

Whose Are You

We all live under the same sky, but we do not all have the same horizon.
—Konrad Adenauer

As an athlete, we are all cognizant of how important it is to have a strong healthy body to be able to perform at our maximum potential. Let me offer this thought to you; how many of you are working on your body so intently that you have neglected your soul. Think about this one day your body will deteriorate and die, while your soul will last forever.

Colossians 1:16 says, "For in Him all things were created: things in heaven and on earth, visible and invisible, whether thrones or powers or rulers or authorities; all things have been created through Him and for Him." *The Ripple Effect* is designed to have you continue to intensely work on your body; development of skills to perform in your sport, become bigger, faster, stronger to become an ultimate competitor but to integrate that work with the intentional development of your soul, your faith, your character, and yourself so in doing so you will ultimately be able to reach significance.

This approach is very different from a conventional program. The program is developed in such a way that you not only learn how to but you begin to employ that knowledge both in terms of performance on the field or court as well as in the classroom, on campus and in the community.

This is *The Ripple Effect to Develop Character and Spiritual Formation*:

> One student athlete with Christian character can improve a team.
> One team with Christian character can improve an athletic program.
> One athletic program with Christian character can impact a community.

From the sideline, to the sidewalk, to significance

One day, your collegiate experience will flash before your eyes. Will it be a highlight film?

Rick Warren makes this statement, "The search for the purpose of life has puzzled people for thousands of years. That is because we typically begin at the wrong starting point—ourselves . . . If you want to know why you were placed on this planet, you must begin with God. You were born by His purpose, for His purpose . . . Focusing on ourselves will never reveal our life's purpose . . . It is only in God that we discover our origin, our identity, our meaning, our purpose, our significance and our destiny."[2]

It is as important for you to determine whose you are while you are determining who you are. So you need to know and understand where you stand with God. Warren commenting from the Bible illustrates whose you are with the following scripture, "It is in Christ that we find out who we are and what we are living for. Long before we first heard of Christ and got our hopes up, He had His eye on us, had designs on us for glorious living, part of the overall purpose He is working out in everything and everyone"[3] (Ephesians 1:11, MSG).

In *The Purpose Driven Life*, Rick Warren says in the first sentence of the book, "IT IS NOT ABOUT YOU." In your development and maturation as a student athlete, it is all about you and your relationship with Christ. It is not about you and your ego or your sense of entitlement, it is about whom you are as a person, about your identity, it is about whose you are, your purpose and being part of something bigger than your-selves as a collegiate student athlete and how you can use the lessons you learn on the sidelines take them to the sidewalk and become a person of significance.

Intercollegiate Athletics exists for stu-dent athletes. It is a privilege and honor to be able to participate and compete in inter-collegiate athletics. Student-athletes are not only expected to be committed academi-cally and athletically but spiritually as well. Athletics are considered a ministry and an expression of God's kingdom. The opportu-nities to learn about oneself, life situations, discipline, teamwork, and the development of one's talents and gifts make intercollegiate athletics an integral part of the overall edu-cational program. The ultimate goal is that the collegiate experience will enable stu-dent athletes' an appropriate balance among these dimensions which will allow a healthy perspective on the use of time and talents as they serve Christ. This approach is to honor the uniqueness of each student athlete and to recognize that each individual is at a dif-ferent point in his or her journey. At the same time, it is important that we begin to develop the potential of each individual to achieve success and establishing significance through the acquisition of skills, values, and principles that will enable them to meet all of life's challenges. Finally, and most import-ant, it is about your faith and your walk with Jesus. Most people can tell you what their faith was when they were growing up, *their parent's faith*, but cannot define *their* faith.

Romans 12:3 says, "I'm speaking to you out of deep gratitude for all that God has given me, and especially as I have respon-sibilities in relation to you. Living then, as every one of you does, in pure grace, it's important that you not misinterpret your-selves as people who are bringing this good-ness to God. No, God brings it all to you. The only accurate way to understand our-selves is by what God is and by what He does for us, not by what we are and what we do for Him."

When God becomes the center of your life you can be begin to discover who you are as a person. Russell Kelfer's poem sums up this up:

You are who you are for a reason.
You are part of an intricate plan.
You are a precious and
perfect unique design,
Called God's special woman or man

You look like you look for a reason.
Our God make no mistake.
He knit you together with the womb,
You are just what He wanted to make

The parents you had were
the ones He chose,
And no matter how you may feel,
They were custom-designed
with God's plan in mind,
and they bear the Master's seal.

No, that trauma you faced is not easy.
And God wept it hurt you so;
but it was allowed to shape your heart
So that into His likeness you would grow.

You are who you are for a reason,
You have been formed by the Master's rod.
You are who you are, beloved,
Because there is a God.

God made you for a purpose. Over two thousand years ago, Jesus went to the cross for you. Ask God to enlarge your life so you can make a greater impact for Him. Do you want more influence? Do you want more responsibility? Do you want an opportunity to have a greater impact? Look at your situation and ask where you are now? What are your boundaries and what do these boundaries include; are you really pursuing your passion earnestly? What is your potential? Do you have a plan to pursue your passion so you can reach your potential as an athlete and person? Are you focusing and establishing your priorities? Jesus provides us this promise He wants you to accept this as a significant opportunity to impact others and use the gifts and talents provided you for His glory.

Perception
The perception is there always will be time.

Passion
Passion is the fuel that helps people nourish and protect their dreams.

Potential
The challenge in determining and reaching your potential is between what you have done and what you are capable of doing.

Priorities
Priorities align what is important to you.

Stat Sheet

Fundamentals: Basic Skills

1. Priorities align what is important to you.
2. Establishing your priorities allow you to focus on what is important so you do not drift through life.
3. As a student athlete, your responsibility and focus is to pursue excellence toward significance.
   - Significance is the management by objectives; it looks beyond the focus on outcomes (scoreboard) to a leadership model that is actually management by values as well as objectives and outcomes. True significance comes when you reach those objectives and outcomes with your values still intact. In achieving significance you put your personal signature is on everything you do. Significance is all about impact.

Discuss what these sentences mean to you?

God's bounty is limited only by us, not by His resources, power, or willingness to give. The true path of significant performance comes as a result of stability and success. Success is building value in you. Significance is creating value in and for others. While you desire to have significant performance, you need a foundation of values or principles to provide security and sustainability for these performances, significance is unsustainable without stability.

- What is your foundation to create value in and for others?

4. To focus and establish priorities you need discipline
    - Define these disciplines in your own words.
        o Discipline of honesty
        o Discipline of self
        o Discipline to respect authority
        o Discipline of habit

Strength and Conditioning Training: Improving Your Shape

1. If we gave an artist a block of granite and asked them to carve a lion, how would the artist do it?
    - The answer is simple an artist with vision would take the chisel and hammer and chip away everything that did not look like a lion.
    - As you establish and develop your priorities you need to "chip away" everything that does not reflect who you are and what you want to become to be able to move toward significance. In other words, you need to determine what is really important to you in your collegiate experience and list them here.
    - In the story that we all have read or seen on television, *The Wizard of Oz*, we find an excellent example to begin with the end in mind and using the characters in the story to begin to develop our true identity.

2. The Oz story is about a dream (Dorothy gets hit on the head and is knocked out). All the characters she encounters are projected parts of herself that she has not integrated.
    - Oz and the Wicked Witch are her rejecting parents
    The Good Witch is an idealized mother
    - The Scarecrow, the Tin Man, and Lion are various parts of Dorothy that she sees as deficient.

3. Each character in the story has some defined qualities that can be identified in each of us. Listed below are the defined qualities of each character.
    - Oz (the wizard) role is defined with power and authority. He feared people getting too close and discovering who he was so he hid in a tower with a bullhorn and barked out orders.
    - The Scarecrow thinks he is not smart enough and wants a brain.
    - The Tin Man believes himself to be heartless and wants a heart.

- The Lion thinks he is a coward and desires courage.

4. In many ways, these characters resemble many of the challenges we face and question ourselves with. Who am I? Who will love me? What can I do with my life? Am I smart or dumb? Am I a good enough athlete? Am I a winner or a loser? Where does God fit in my life?

5. *We want you to select one of these characters and defined the qualities that you believe you possess and explain why as a way of helping you decide what is important to you in establishing your priorities.*

Game Day: Performing with Excellence

1. What is identity?
   - Identity is defined as a condition of being oneself and not another

2. Look at the types of identity
   - Lost identity
   - Confused identity
   - False ID
   - Identity theft
   - Allow others create your ID for you

3. Why is it important to have a knowledge of your identity
   - Knowing your identity demonstrates spiritual identity
     o Who am I?

   o What meaning do I have?
   o Where am I going?
   - Knowing who you are
   - Knowing who God made you to be
   - Knowing your true identity
     o Not the identity your parent gave you
     o Not the identity society gave you
     o Learning the identity your father in heaven gave you.
     o What does understanding who you are do for you?
   - Builds confidence
   - Lowers insecurities
   - Develops stability
     o How you develop stability in your life so you do not let people run over you because you know who you are and you do not let them determine who you should be.
   - **Who are you letting define your identity (establish your priorities):**

4. Our task is to put our life priorities into action. To do this your priorities need to include the following:
   - They need to be principle and value centered. This allows you to use your time on what is really important and effective for your purpose.

Everything is not really, really important.

- They need to have balance. This identifies the various constituents that you need to support. There is not enough time to do everything.
- They need to have a spiritual context. Many times in our busyness we tend to give God our leftovers.

- **Using these criteria have you established your priorities so that you can perform with excellence and reach significance? If you have priorities, what are they? If you do not have priorities, why not?**

Endnotes

[1] Rick Warren. *What on Earth Am I Here For?* Zondervan: 2013, 36.
[2] Rick Warren. *What on Earth Am I Here For?* Zondervan: 2013, 21–22.
[3] Rick Warren. *What on Earth Am I Here For?* Zondervan: 2013, 24.

The Power of Christ

The life of every living creature and the spirit in every human body are in His hands.
—Job 12:10

This is the component to *The Ripple Effect* in finding your purpose or identity that some people do not wish to explore or miss entirely. You can establish your passion for something, begin to develop your potential, and establish priorities that can lead to some success without the power of Christ in your life.

> You can succeed momentarily
> by what you know;
> You can succeed temporarily
> by what you can do;
> A few of you can succeed
> permanently by what you are;
> But for you to have a significant
> impact with your life;
> You need to live in the light of
> eternity with the power of Christ.

Without God, life has no purpose, and without purpose, life has no meaning. Without meaning life has no significance or hope."[1] "God can do anything, you know—far more than you could ever imagine or guess or request in your wildest dreams! He does it not by pushing us around but by working within us, His Spirit deeply and gently within us" (Ephesians 3:20–21).

What drives your life? God wants you to be part of His family. He does not want you to be His servant, slave, soldier, worker, or employer. He wants you to be in His fam-ily, His teammate, His son or daughter. "For God so loved the world that He gave His one and only Son, that whoever believes in Him shall not perish but have eternal life" (John 3:16).

You were created to become like Christ. "In all creation, only human beings are made 'in God's image.' This is a great privilege and gives us dignity. We do not know all this phase covers, but we do know some of the aspects it includes: Like God, we are spiritual beings—our spirits are immortal and will outlast our earthly bodies; we are intellectual—we can think, reason, and solve problems; like God, we are relational—we can give and receive love; and we have a moral consciousness—we can discern right from wrong, which makes us accountable to God."[2] The full image of God looks like Christ.

God wants you to mature spiritually and become more like Christ. Ephesians 4:22–24 (MSG) says, "Take on an entirely new way of life—a God-fashioned life, a life renewed from the inside and working itself into your conduct as God accurately reproduces His character in you." However, becoming like Christ does not mean losing your personality or becoming a mindless clone. God created your uniqueness, so He certainly does not want to destroy it. Christ-likeness is all about transforming your character, not your personality. God wants you to bear His image and His likeness but He does not want you to become a god; He wants you to become godly, taking on the values, attitudes, and character of Christ His son.

God loves us so much that He sent Jesus to live amongst us, to die for your sins, and be resurrected so that you might have eternal life. What a sacrifice of love. God wants a relationship with you. In developing your identity in your collegiate experience these three basic needs need to be met: all of these needs are about a relationship—Christ provides the best opportunity for a significant relationship; (1) for someone to believe in you and to affirm and validate your inherent value and potential. God wants you to love Him, where there is love there is encouragement and support; (2) a belief system that develops into a lifestyle for you to make positive choices; where is there a stronger belief system than the Bible? The proof is that Jesus has existed for over two thousand years; (3) a place to belong—a community (team) built on well-defined principles with expectations and boundaries that provide structure and safeguards. God wants you to be a part of His family, to be a teammate, a son, or daughter.

What are the benefits of being God's (Christ's) teammate? Identity is found in your relationships. Relationship means being tied to another person. In the case of your family these relationships would be with your mother, father, and siblings. In God's family, He would be the Father and you the son/daughter. Relationships provide connections with other people. Your physical family provides a model for God's family, your spiritual family. In God's family your weaknesses, mistakes, warts, or sins do not define you anymore. You are a child of God who is capable of using your gifts and talents for His glory.

With God as your teammate you have stability and support. In the Bible, the body of Christ is referred to as a temple.

"In Christ the whole building is **joined together** and rises to become a **holy temple** in the Lord. And in Him you too are **being built together** to become a **dwelling** in which God lives by His Spirit" (Ephesians 2:21–22, NIV). In a building, all parts are necessary and they must be connected to each other for the building to stand. Spare parts are not part of the building because they are not connected, they cannot stand alone. Stability in life is important because it overcomes loneliness and insecurity. "I want us to help each other with the faith we have. Your faith will help me, and my faith will help you" (Romans 1:12, NCV).

Being a teammate of Christ allows you to discover your unique value, your capacity. "Just as there are many parts to our bodies, so it is with Christ's body. We are all parts of it, and it takes every one of us to make it complete, for we each have different work to do. So we belong to each other and each of us needs all the others" (Romans 12:4–5). A team has many parts all different where everyone is needed; all have roles and all roles are equal. As teammates we belong to each other and we all need each other. "If your foot says, 'I am not a part of the body because I am not a hand,' that does not make it any less a part of the body. And if your ear says, 'I am not part of the body because I am only an ear and not an eye,' would that make it any less a part of the body?" (1 Corinthians 12:15–16, NLT). Every teammate is important. Some are more visible than others; you cannot do it on your own.

Due to the nature of God, He provides His teammates with a level of confidence. This level of confidence provides a level of security to you because you have someone that cares for you and about you. "Encourage each other and give each other strength" (Thessalonians 5:11). A teammate is someone that walks into your life when others walk out. This provides a powerful feeling of confidence and security. With Christ as a teammate you can move from being dependent, all about me and my needs, to independence, making your own decisions but open to the promises of Christ, to interdependence, understanding your identity or purpose and the ability to live it. "Have confidence in your leaders and submit to their authority, because they keep watch over you as those who must give an account. Do this so that their work will be a joy, not a burden, for that would be of no benefit to you" (Hebrews 13:17, MSG).

Finally, being in God's family, being your teammate, your life becomes more productive, fruitful; "A branch cannot produce fruit if it is severed from the vine, and you cannot be fruitful apart from me. I am the vine and you are the branches. Those who remain in me and I in them, will produce much fruit. But apart from me you can do nothing" (John 15:4–5, NLT). Disconnected branches cannot bear fruit; fruitfulness makes your life count. *Being a teammate of Christ gives you a power to live on (Christ), people to live with (relationships), principles to live by (core values), a plan to live out (**GOLD PRIDE**), and a purpose to live for (your destiny).*

"Follow me" the first words of Christ to His disciples. Great teams have both a good balance between leading and follow-ing. Following has a negative connotation in our present society especially in athletics. Many athletes feel they need to be in charge and have the control. However, to become a great leader you need to first humble yourself to be a quality follower. You cannot possibly be a good leader for God until you have first become a good follower of God. There is a great promise in John 12:26 that God will honor those who serve and follow Christ. David tells us in Psalm 23 that as we follow God, goodness and mercy will follow us all the days of our lives. Luke 14:27 says, "Whoever does not carry the cross and follow me cannot be my disciple." There is a difference between "traveling with" and "following" Jesus. Who has your true allegiance?

"The most damaging aspect of contemporary living is short-term thinking. To make the most of your life, you must keep the vision of eternity continually in your mind and the value of it in your heart. There is far more to life than the here and now. Today is the visible tip of the iceberg. Eternity is all the rest you do not see under the surface."[3] Your spiritual formation is meant to deepen your understanding of your purpose, your role within groups (teams) and to encourage you to seek ways to serve and lead. If you understand the "who" and "why" of having the power of Christ in your life, you will soon discover the blessing He has for you. "Everything comes from God alone. Everything lives by His power, and everything is for His glory" (Romans 11:36). Using your gifts and talents for God's glory is the greatest impact you can have with your life.

Who We Choose to Follow

Every person on this earth, including you, has the potential to make a difference. But you can do it only if you believe in yourself and are willing to give yourself away to others.
—James Maxwell

Who you choose to follow will determine to a large degree what you become. God loves to hear your heart. Nothing is too big or too small. It is easy for all of us to turn inward and start thinking life is all about us. Life does not revolve around your dreams, your agenda, your fulfillment, your significance and security, your relationships and so on. *It is ultimately about God; that singular focus transforms every relationship and every thought.*

Those who read truth are more likely to live it out. In addition, you can learn from someone else but you cannot get confidence from them. You can learn from them but convictions are born out of self-study when the Spirit of God takes truth and makes it real in your heart. The Christian life is a relationship. It is about being united with Christ, both in His death and in His resurrection. Life is no longer about simply going to church or being moral or nice; it is a relationship that you live out in a spirit of gratitude. The true test of spiritual maturity is not knowledge but love for God and love for others. The test of love for God is whether at any given moment you can say "thank you" for what is happening in your life and the test of love for others is whether you are free from envy. This is the key to **GOLD PRIDE**.

What is the value of prayer in determining who you are/whose you are? Prayer should not be the last resort it should be the first choice. When you ask God to intervene in our lives or in someone else's life, you are actually admitting your own weakness. You come to God because you know you cannot handle whatever situation you are in. On the other hand, when you do not pray very much, you are really saying that even though the Lord created the universe, you think you can handle your problems and guide yourself through life. It means that you are putting a lot of stock in your own intelligence, resources, and power quietly claiming your own sufficiency. Genuine prayer acknowledges who God is and your need for Him. This is a sign of humility. Remember, humility is not thinking less of you. It is thinking of others instead and acting in their best interest instead of your own.

God puts great people in your life so you can learn from them. A master's ceiling can become His disciple's floor if the disciple knows how to absorb the lessons of His master's life. History is full of people who connected themselves with great people and eventually rose to their level of maturity. A simple fact of human nature is that you begin to take on the attributes of people you spend the most time with. Thank God for what you have rather than what you did not get. Need to spend time thanking God for the blessings you did receive. Make your life a blazing blessing. Express appreciation for a lifetime. Deal constructively with the damage so you can grow.

How do you know which people to pursue? You need to look in the rearview mirror. When look back to see how and why God used certain people to develop your character, you begin to notice patterns. You need to create your own Mt. Rushmore. Identify those few people whose influence in your life is positive and indelible. The people you will always remember because they inspired you and taught you about life.

When you have looked in the rearview mirror and reflected on your Mt. Rushmore of great influences, you have a better idea of whom to pursue next. Look out the windshield to see the people God has placed on your horizon, knowing that He put some of them there to mold you into the person He wants you to be.

Anais Nin said, "We don't see things as they are; we see them as we are." What people believe (think) about themselves determines how they live and what they choose to become. Some people believe who they are is genetically determined, and others believe who they are is acquired through their effort and experiences. Experts indicate that much of what is causing an identity crisis in our college-age students today is a lack of meaningful relationships and connections with moral and spiritual meaning. What you believe about yourself, whom you believe in are important factors in finding your identity. "Do not let anyone capture you with empty philosophies and high sounding nonsense that come from human thinking (expectations) and from spiritual powers of this world, rather than from Christ" (Colossians 2:8). Jesus developed relationships. He offered praise, healing, peace, and grace. Jesus was a sacrificing, serving savior.

"Fix our eyes on Jesus, the author and perfecter of our faith, who for the joy set before Him endured the cross, scorning its shame, and sat down at the right hand of the throne of God" (Hebrew 12:2).

Things to keep in mind as you formulate **who you are/whose you are** and your ability to make positive choices that will provide the direction for your life:

1. What Jesus did for you on the cross; He did not deny you. Do not focus on where you are in your faith or what you have done in your past, focus on the price He paid for you.
    *   You need to live in the light of eternity not the here and now.

2. At some point you will have to give an account to God of what you have done with the gifts and talent He gave you. To follow Jesus you need to keep your eyes on Him just as in athletics you need to keep your eyes on the ball.
    *   It is not what you are living for but who you are living for. Do things His way with Him as your teammate

3. Integrity is more important than popularity. It is not what you are going through but what you are going to, the Power of Christ.
    *   Would you rather walk through life with God without all the answers or walk

through life without God and have all the answers?

God doesn't want your "reasons" . . . He wants your obedience.

Remember

If you want to be distressed—look within
If you want to be defeated—look back
If you want to be distracted—look around
If you want to be dismayed—look ahead
If you want to be delivered—look up

Perception
The perception is there always will be time.

Passion
Passion is the fuel that helps people nourish and protect their dreams

Potential
The challenge in determining and reaching your potential is between what you have done and what you are capable of doing.

Priorities
Priorities align what is important to you

Power of Christ
You were created to become like Christ.

Stat Sheet

Fundamentals: Basic Skills

1. Without God, life has no purpose, and without purpose, life has no meaning. Without meaning life has no significance or hope.
2. What are the benefits of being God's (Christ's) teammate?
3. There is a difference between "traveling with" and "following" Jesus. What is the difference in your mind?

Strength and Conditioning Training: Improving Your Shape

1. God puts great people in our lives so we can learn from them
   - A master's ceiling can become His disciple's floor if the disciple knows how to absorb the lessons of His master's life.
     o What does this mean to you in your life?
   - Look in the rearview mirror.
     o Who is on your Mt. Rushmore? List five and explain about one.
   - Look out the windshield
     o Who you choose to follow will determine to a large degree what you become.
   - Who has God placed on your horizon that will help mold your collegiate experience? Give an example in your life where you applied this concept.

Game Day: Performing with Excellence

1. Dan and his wife Christine began to live each day with tremendous clarity and love when they found out that she had been diagnosed with terminal cancer.
   - When it was near the end Joe a friend of both Dan and Christine finally got up enough courage to ask Christine this question,
     - "What does it feel like to live each day knowing you are dying?"
     - Her response was, "Joe what does it feel like to live each day pretending that you are not?"
   - One of the most powerful questions for focusing on where the power of Christ fits in your life is asking yourself, "What would I be doing with my time if I knew I had only six healthy months to live?"
     - Focus is the beginning of power.
   - It can immediately cause you to reorganize your priorities.
   - When Jesus, looks at you He will ask you one question:
     - "What do you want me to do for you?"
   - This is a question Jesus asked again and again in His ministry
   - **If Jesus asked you that question now what would your response be?**
     - It is up to you to decide on who you want to be and what you want to be about in this world.
   - Need an understanding of what your passion is and how your passion is related to your priorities to have focus.
   - Need to understand that Jesus cannot use His power for you until you know how you want Him to be involved and the direction you want to go.
   - It is first your choice, then His power
   - Are you using the power of Christ in your life? If so how? If not, are you willing to find that power?

Endnotes

1   Rick Warren. *What on Earth Am I Here For?* Zondervan: 2013, 34.
2   Rick Warren. *What on Earth Am I Here For?* Zondervan: 2013, 171.
3   Rick Warren. *What on Earth Am I Here For?* Zondervan: 2013, 171.

Section III

The Rules
of the Road

Core Values Defined

Your journey in life is a series of choices. When you travel or drive across the country you would use a road atlas (GPS) to guide you. These maps use lines on paper to represent physical roads. Knowing your ultimate destination, you would plot a course to get you from where you are to where you want to get. The journey of your collegiate experience works the same way. You navigate your life by the choices you make. Each choice on your travel map brings about a specific outcome; a series of good choices will take you in a positive direction, while poor choices, even small ones, can lead you to unhappiness. A knowledge and understanding of the "rules of the road" presented in section III provide you a foundation to make choices that can help you chart the future course in direction where you want to go.

Defining the Core Values of Gold Pride

GOLD PRIDE is established through the development of core covenants (values/standards) that become convictions by each team and team members using the first two commandments intertwined with the values of Integrity, Respect, Responsibility, Sportsmanship and Servant Leadership.

GOLD PRIDE encompasses the first two commandments

1. Love God
   - "My food . . . is to do the will of Him who sent me." (John 4:34)
   - "The one who sent me is with me; He has not left me alone, for I always do what pleases Him" (John 8:29).
   - You are designed by God for God—you have a purpose.
      o Do what is pleasing to God.
      o Being responsible for what you know.
      o God will ask you what you did with the gifts He gave you.

2. Love people
   - "The son of Man did not come to be served but to serve and to give His life as a ransom for many" (Mark 10:15).
   - Serve others—be a servant leader.

Live Five Core Values

Integrity: Know and do what is right.

Respect: Treating others the way you want to be treated.

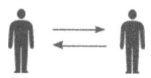

Responsibility: Embrace the role you play on the team.

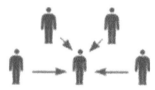

Sportsmanship: Bring the best to all competition.

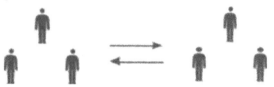

Servant-leadership: Serve the common good of the team.

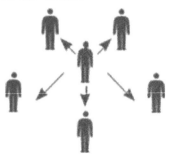

GOLD PRIDE uses these five core values to establish significance:

1. Integrity
   - Know and do what is right.

- Positive internal traits that guide behavior.
- Who you are as a person (being true to your values and convictions).
- Integrity is your ability to be trustworthy with yourself and your teammates.
- It determines what your signature is worth.
- Integrity in the NAIA model of Live 5: just, honest, consistent, courageous, and disciplined.

Respect
- Treating others the way you want to be treated.
- Respect is valuing the person or situation that stands before you.
   o In an athletic setting the person standing before you could be the coach, a teammate, an opponent, an officials, or a spectator.
- Respect is the baseline for living by a higher standard.
- Respect is the value you place on something.
- Respect shapes how you see any activity in which you will participate.
- Respect in the NAIA model of Live 5: tolerant, considerate, attentive, encouraging, and appreciative.

Responsibility

- Embrace the role you play on the team.
- The social force that binds you to the group or team.
- Responsibility is a social contract among a group's members to act in a manner that leads to greater group success.
- All great teams throughout history have had one thing in common: unity of purpose.
- To be accountable to your values and convictions.
- The relationships you have with yourself will determine the relationship you have with others.
- Responsibility in the NAIA model of Live 5: conscientious, accountable, helpful, persevering, and reliable.

Sportsmanship

- Bring the best to all competition.
- Is following the rules, spirit, and etiquette of athletic competition as well as those regulations that govern other areas of your life.
  - o How you relate to your opponents in the athletic arena and how you relate to requirements you face with your career, in your family, or with the general public.
  - o It demonstrates both internal and external character.
- It is both a product of internal traits such as obedience, fairness, and justice, as well as external traits such as hospitality and humility.
- It is following the rules of a contest and demonstrating a concern about the spirit and etiquette of how the contest was played or administered.
- It is having the discipline to do what is right when it is right.
  - o You can adjust your actions to meet to your principles, or you can adjust principles to meet your actions.
  - o Discipline is a positive for an athlete.
- It is establishing boundaries that help modify behavior.
  - o It is not a passive activity of acceptance.
  - o It is a positive statement that an individual student athlete or team is disciplined enough to maintain perspective and poise, do what is best for their teammates and act correctly even when others do not.
- Sportsmanship in the NAIA model of Live 5: cooperative, fair, gracious, honorable, and humble.

Servant Leadership

- Serve the common good of the team.
- Servant-leadership encourages individuals to serve others while staying focused on achieving results in line with the team's values.
  - o Becoming selfless.
  - o Being a part of something bigger than yourself by developing a great team.
- This core value demonstrates both internal and external character.
  - o In an athletic setting a team's chances for success are increased when its members become servant-leaders.
  - o A team made up of servant-leaders trusts their coach to make the best decision for the team.
  - o Whether you are the star of the team or the person that makes the star better each and every day in practice your role is important.
  - o Understanding the role you play on the team and accepting that role demonstrates servant-leadership.
- Servant Leadership in the NAIA model of Live 5: empowering, visionary, interconnected, generous, and assertive.

From the sideline, to the sidewalk, to significance

The essence of the NAIA Champions of Character program and **GOLD PRIDE** is to change the culture of sport. We still want to be competitive; still want to get the enjoyment from competing in the game of your passion; still want you to become the best you can become as an athlete and person, but we want you to consider being part of a standard greater than victory and having standards (core covenants) that will allow you to develop habits that will set you and your teams apart from those in your conference. We want your actions to meet your principles (standards)

The Commandments

Love God with all your heart, soul, and mind. Love your neighbor as yourself.

If you are a people pleaser, you will not honor God because you are not following His purpose for your life so you will dishonor both the first and second commandments.

Is there something more important than God in your life? If so that is your God. To honor the first commandment, you dishonor God if He is not first in your life, you cannot have another idol. In loving God are you living your life from His smile because you are in His will, He loves you though Christ or are you living your life for His smile always attempting to please Him with your own agenda?

"I want you to show love, not offer sacrifices. I want you to know me more than I want burnt offerings" (Hosea 6:6). "Can you sense God's passion for you in this verse? God deeply loves you and desires your love in return. He longs for you to know Him and spend time with Him. This is why learning to love God and be loved by Him should be the greatest objective of your life. Nothing else comes close in importance. Jesus called it the greatest commandment. He said, 'Love your God with all your heart and with all your soul and with all you mind. This is the first and greatest commandment.'"[1]

You were made in the image of God so He could love you. This is the reason for the first commandment—love God with all your heart, soul, and mind. Everything was created for God to love and for us to love. Love validates your faith. 1 John 4:8 says, "Whoever does not love does not know God, because God is love." Love integrates your life; provides you a center. Love is more important than anything else. Love acts like the thread that binds everything together. It is what ties everything completely together. Love lives on forever. "Three things will continue forever: faith, hope and love. And the greatest of these is love" (1 Corinthians 13:13). The best way to leave a legacy is to love people.

Life is about learning to love, God and others. Love is the lesson of life. There are four ways to live an intentional life of love. **Live life passionately in love**; to do this, you need to get out of your comfort zone and into a compassion zone. **Love completely**; love people where they are at like Christ did. There are three things to help you love completely, say it now, express your love, show it now with hugs, share it now, take time with those you love. **Live humbly in love**; humility is a choice. "When you do things, do not let selfishness or pride be your guide. Instead, be humble and give honor to others rather than yourself. Do not be interested only in your own life, but be interested in the lives of others. In your life you must think and act like Christ Jesus" (Philippians 2:3–5). **You need to become selfless in love**. "Whoever wants to become a leader among you must be your servant" (Mark 10:43). **Learn to laugh at yourself**. James 4:6 says, "God opposes the proud and give grace to the humble." "Pride leads to disgrace but with humility comes wisdom" (Proverbs 11:2). Finally, you need **to lead boldly in love**; you must choose to value what God values. Remember, God wants all of you. The best expression of love is time. Love is spelled *time*. The most desired gift of love is focused attention, giving time to someone in your life. We all have different gifts, talents, money; however, all of us all have the same amount of time. The essence of relationships is how much we give of ourselves to each other. "The only thing that counts is faith expressing itself through love" (Galatians 5:6).

God's love is not based on what you do but on His love for you because He created you. God loves you on your good days and your bad days. Ephesians 3:17–19 says, "I pray that Christ will be more and more at home in your hearts as you trust in Him. May your roots go down deep into the soul of God's marvelous love? And may you have the power to understand, as all God's people should, how wide, how long, how high, how deep, His love really is. May you experience the love of Christ, though it is so great you will never fully understand it?" God's love is wide enough to be everywhere, but you need to be tuned into God to realize this. Long enough to last forever; understand human love wears out, God's does not. His love is deep enough to handle anything and high enough to overlook your sins and mistakes. Most of us have head knowledge of God's love but we do not have heart knowledge so we miss the joy of a relationship with Him by eighteen inches, the distance from your head to your heart.

"Go after a life of love as if your life depended on it—because it does. Give yourselves to the gifts God gives you" (1 Corinthians 14:1–2). God put you on earth for a test to see if you can trust Him and learn to love. The highest form of love is when you act in love when you do not feel like it because God is love and wants you to be like Him. During your collegiate experience you need to learn how much God loves you.

The Basics of Love

1. We love because God loves us
   - "We love because God first loved us" (1 John 4:19).
   - "Love comes from God . . . for God is love" (1 John 4:7–7).
   - "We know and rely on the love God has for us" (1 John 4:16a).
     - o Cannot love others unless you first feel love.
     - o This comes from the love of God.

2. Love is a choice and a commitment
   - "Choose to love the Lord your God . . . and commit yourself to Him . . ." (Deuteronomy 30:20).
     - o Attraction and arousal are emotions and not a choice.
     - o Cannot command an emotion.
     - o Loving when you do not feel like it is the highest form of love

3. Love is an action not just an emotion
   - "Let us not love with words or tongue but with actions and in truth" (1 John 3:18).
     - o Love is something you do—it is a behavior.
     - o Love can cause or create feelings but it is not an emotion.
     - o It is easier to act your way to a feeling than it is to feel your way into an action.

4. Love is a skill you can learn.
   - "Dear friends, let us practice loving each other, for love comes from God and those who are loving and kind show that they are the children of God, and that they are getting to know Him better" (1 John 4:7).

- "Practice these things and devote yourself to them, in order that your progress may be seen by all" (1 Timothy 4:15).

5. Love is a habit.
   - "Continue to love each other with true Christian love" (Hebrews 13:1).
     o Need to habitually display love (character)
   - Cannot tell the truth 90 percent of the time.
     o If love is not a habit, you only love those that love you—you need to love all—love needs to become a lifestyle.

Bill McCartney, a former leader in Promise Keepers said, "Any time you devalue people, you question God's creation. You can connect with people only if you value them. In addition, being genuine (authentic) is very important in loving others as you love yourself.

For others to love you they need to know and see the real you.

When you want to connect with another person, start where both of you agree; this is common ground." James Maxwell "describes the following sequence in connecting with others, feel, felt, and found. First try to sense what they feel and acknowledge and validate the feelings. If you have had similar feelings in the past then share with them about how you have also felt the same way before. Finally, share with them what you have found that has helped you work through the feelings."[2]

In learning to love others as you love yourself, you need to realize that you cannot control people or force them to change. In addition, you need to realize that imperfect people (like yourself) sin and cause damage. Sin is disobedient to God's way; it causes damage to you and others. Therefore as you begin to connect with others (love them) your attitude is very important. You need an attitude of compassion. You need to respond to others with the realization of you can only control your response not theirs. Respond with God's power instead of your power; respond with the fruits of the spirit love, joy, peace, long-suffering, kindness, goodness, faithfulness, gentleness, and self-control. The power of your words is paramount in loving others.

The symbol that Jesus died on the cross is not the cross, not a fish, not a dove; it needs to be our love for Him and His love for us. "So this is my prayer; that your love will flourish and that you will not only love much but well. **Learn to love appropriately.** You need to use your head and test your feelings so that your love is sincere and intelligent, not sentimental gush. Live a lover's life, circumspect and exemplary, a life Jesus will be proud of bountiful in fruits from the soul, making Jesus Christ attractive to all, getting everyone involved in the glory and praise of God" (Philippians 1:9–11).

Rules of the Road

**The Commandments
Life is about learning to
love, God, and others.**

Stat Sheet

Fundamentals: Basic Skills

1. The Pharisees asked Jesus, "Which is the greatest commandment in the Law?" Jesus response was the first commandment, "'You shall love your Lord your God with all your heart, and with all your soul, and with all your mind.' This is the great and foremost commandment. The second is like the first, 'You shall love your neighbor as yourself.'"

2. Is there something more important than God in your life? If so that is your God. To honor the first commandment you dishonor God if He is not first in your life, you cannot have another idol.

Are you attempting to live your life from God's smile (because you are in His will) or for His smile (because of your performance)?

Strength and Conditioning Training: Improving Your Shape

1. Rick Warren said, "You cannot arrive at your life's purpose (who you are—your identity) by starting with a focus on yourself. You must begin with God, your Creator. You exist only because God wills that you exist. You were made by God for God . . . It is only in God that we discover our origin, our identity, our meaning, our purpose our significance and our destiny."[3]

   • "How are you discovering the purpose you were created for? Is Christ part of the equation?

Game Day: Performing with Excellence

1. How are the two greatest commandments making a difference in your life today?

2. How can the two greatest commandments be used to improve you as a person of significance?

Endnotes

[1] Rick Warren. *What on Earth Am I Here For?* Zondervan: 2013, 72.

[2] James Maxwell. *Becoming a Person of Influence.* Nashville: Thomas Nelson, 1997, 170.

[3] Rick Warren. *What on Earth Am I Here For?* Zondervan: 2013, 22.

Integrity

The need for integrity today is perhaps as great as it has ever been. It is absolutely essential for anyone who desires to be a person of character.

Integrity—what a great word and a great core value; integrity is a combination of all inward traits that build upon one another to determine who you are. It is a choice of correct behavior displayed in small daily decisions. Do your actions follow your words? Do your actions follow your beliefs; are you walking your talk? Does your yes mean yes, and your no mean no?

Integrity is about the relationship you have both with yourself and with others. It means being just, to treat yourself and everyone else fairly. "Integrity commits itself to character over personal gain, to people over things, to service over power, to principle over convenience, to the long view over the immediate."[1]

Integrity requires that you be honest as you practice and compete. Do not wield the truth like a sword to degrade others; instead, hold the truth like a torch to light the way to everyone's best performance. Like a ship, the structural integrity of an individual depends upon the material used to build it and the people who guide its construction. Linked to moral character integrity might be described as an individual's inside identity. Integrity displays a depth in character; the depth is shown in honesty, sincerity, reliability, respect, humility, and loyalty.

Integrity requires you to be consistent—where your actions meet your principles in every situation inside and outside the athletic arena. "When people around you know that you are a person of integrity, they know that you want to influence them because of the opportunity to add value to their lives. They do not have to worry about your motives."[2]

To be a person of integrity takes courage. Often times the perceptions of courage needs to be changed; courage is not always something that is a dramatic or newsworthy event, more often, real courage can be seen in small decisions and choices that individual athletes make on a daily basis, to not letting their teammates down. Integrity resolves around the degree to which a person maintains the courage of his convictions. This kind of courage takes persistence to keep believing in yourself and resilience to keep picking yourself up after every setback, every stumble, every fail. Take pride in yourself. Be your own person. Do not do things because everyone else does them. Do not be part of the crowd just to be a part. Dare to be different. Jack Lambert once said, "Never be afraid to stand up for what you believe to be right, even when it means standing alone."

"The bottom line when it comes to integrity is that it allows others to trust you. And without trust, you have nothing. Trust is the single most important factor in personal and professional relationships."[3] Trustworthy people have integrity that fosters trusting relationships; it is your ability as an individual to establish trustworthiness with yourself as well as your teammates and coaches. Trustworthiness of self is your ability to trust yourself to be responsible and accountable. The level of cooperation on any team increases tremendously as the level of trust rises. "At one time you could assume that others would trust you until you gave them a reason not to. But today with most people, you must prove your trustworthiness first . . . Trust comes from others only when you exemplify solid character."[4]

Finally, integrity requires you to be disciplined; to be dedicated and self-controlled even when challenged. "It is almost impossible to overstate the impact of integrity in the lives of people. You probably remember the Tylenol scare from years ago. Several people were poisoned to death, and investigators traced the cause to contaminated Tylenol capsules. John's friend Don Meyer sent him a commentary on the incident. Here is what it said:

Some years earlier in their mission statement, they had a line saying they would "operate with honesty and integrity." Several weeks before the Tylenol incident, the president of Johnson and Johnson sent a memo to all presidents of divisions of the company asking if they were abiding by and if they believed in the mission statement. All of the presidents came back with an affirmative answer.

Reportedly, within an hour of the Tylenol crisis, the president of the company ordered all capsules off the shelf knowing it was a $100 million decision.

When reporters asked how he could decide so easily and rapidly on such a major decision, his reply was, "I was practicing what we agreed on in our mission statement."

At the bottom of the commentary, Don Meyer wrote this note: "John, it is always easy to do right when you know ahead of time what you stand for."

What is true for Johnson and Johnson (the Tylenol Company) is true for you. If you know what you stand for and act accordingly, people can trust you. You are a model of the character and consistency that other people admire and want to emulate.[5]

Rules of the Road

The Commandments
Life is about learning to love, God, and others.

Integrity
To know and do what is right

Stat Sheet

Fundamentals: Basic Skills

1. Integrity what a great word and a great core value; integrity is a combination of all inward traits that build upon one another to determine who you are.
2. "Integrity commits itself to character over personal gain, to people over things, to service over power, to principle over convenience, to the long view over the immediate."
3. "The bottom line when it comes to integrity is that it allows others to trust you. And without trust, you have nothing. Trust is the single most important factor in personal and professional relationships."
4. Integrity determines what your signature is worth; your yes means yes and your no means no.

5. Integrity in the NAIA model of Live 5: just, honest, consistent, courageous, and disciplined.

6. All of the following are traits or qualities of integrity. Pick one and discuss how it is seen in your life?

   • Integrity requires that you be honest in practice and as you compete.

   • Integrity requires you to be consistent, where your actions meet your principles in every situation inside and outside of the athletic arena.

   • To be a person of integrity takes courage.

   • The bottom line when it comes to integrity is that it allows others to trust you.

   • Integrity requires you to be disciplined; to be dedicated and self-controlled even when challenged.

Strength and Conditioning Training: Improving Your Shape

1. "For the LORD gives wisdom; from His mouth come knowledge and understanding; He stores up sound wisdom for the upright; He is a shield to those who walk in integrity, guarding the paths of justice and watching over the way of His saints" (Proverbs 2:6–8).

The Duck and the Devil

There was a little boy visiting his grandparents on their farm He was given a slingshot to play with out in the woods. He practiced in the woods; but he could never hit the target. Getting a little discouraged, he headed back for dinner. As he was walking back he saw Grandma's pet duck. Just out of impulse, he let the slingshot fly, hit the duck square in the head, and killed it. He was shocked and grieved! In a panic, he hid the dead duck in the wood pile only to see his sister watching! Sally had seen it all but she said nothing. After lunch the next day, Grandma said, "Sally, let's wash the dishes." But Sally said, "Grandma, Johnny told me he wanted to help in the kitchen." Then she whispered to him, "Remember the duck?" So Johnny did the dishes. Later that day, Grandpa asked if the children wanted to go fishing and Grandma said, "I'm sorry but I need Sally to help make supper." Sally just smiled and said, "Well that's all right because Johnny told me he wanted to help" She whispered again, "Remember the duck?" So Sally went fishing and Johnny stayed to help. After several days of Johnny doing both his chores and Sally's, he finally couldn't stand it any longer. He came to Grandma and confessed that he had killed the duck Grandma knelt down, gave him a hug and said, "Sweetheart, I know. You see, I was standing at the window and I saw the whole thing, but because I love you, I forgave you. I was just wondering how long you would let Sally make a slave of you."

Thought for the day and every day thereafter?

Whatever is in your past, whatever you have done and whatever the devil keeps throwing in your face (lying, cheating, debt, fear, bad habits, hatred, anger, bitterness, etc.) . . .
Whatever it is . . . You need to know that God was standing at the window and He saw the whole thing.
He has seen your whole life.
He wants you to know that HE LOVES YOU and that you are forgiven.
He's just wondering how long you will let the devil make a slave of you
The great thing about God is that when you ask for forgiveness, He not only forgives, but He forgets. It is by God's grace and mercy that we are saved.

Go ahead and make the difference in someone's life today. Share this with a friend and always remember:
God is at the window!
When Jesus died on the cross
He was thinking of you!

2. **Who in your life do you need to forgive because you did not demonstrate integrity? How can you grow from this experience?**

Game Day: Performing with Excellence
Using the NAIA model for **LIVE 5** write a short paragraph on what *integrity* means to you at this time in your collegiate experience and how you might intentionally make this core value part of your lifestyle

Endnotes

1   James Maxwell. *Becoming a Person of Influence.* Nashville: Thomas Nelson, 1997, 21.
2   James Maxwell. *Becoming a Person of Influence.* Nashville: Thomas Nelson, 1997, 26–27.
3   James Maxwell. *Becoming a Person of Influence.* Nashville: Thomas Nelson, 1997, 27.
4   James Maxwell. *Becoming a Person of Influence.* Nashville: Thomas Nelson, 1997, 27.
5   James Maxwell. *Becoming a Person of Influence.* Nashville: Thomas Nelson, 1997, 32.

Respect

Respect by Don Wilson

Respect is a lesson that
everyone should learn
Respect must be given before
an expected return
Respect is something that's given for free
Respect is about us and never about me
Respect is the basis on which
relationships are founded
Respect is the anchor that keeps
a person well-grounded
Respect builds the character
and defines who we are
Respect sets the standard and raises the bar
Respect is magnanimous and helps to fulfill
Respect is the partner that
sits with good will
Respect is like honey so sweet it's perceived
Respect a taste to savor for
when it's received

Respect is the baseline for living by a higher standard. Respect begins with tolerance. In order to respect others, you first need to accept everyone's right to be treated fairly and empathetically. The opportunity to participate as a student athlete provides you with an opportunity to build self-respect while earning the respect of those you encounter. You need to learn to respect for yourself; learn to understand what your gifts and talents are to establish your potential. You build confidence as you learn about yourself and actively pursue the challenges presented to you. You need to learn respect for others, to recognize the dignity of others and affirm the diversity of their gifts. These would include your mentors (coaches, professors, and administrators), colleagues and peers, parents and siblings, teammates, and opponent in competition. You need to respect property that include facilities on campus, facilities on others campuses, equipment, and your personal property. The sport in which you participate needs to be respected. You must have a high value for competition, the game officials are part of the game, respect their place in the game, compete with passion, play the game to win but accept victory with humility and defeat with dignity, and honor your sport with your best effort in each practice and game. You need to understand the privilege you have to be an athlete. Train your body and mind to the rigors of competition. Provide your body with the proper rest and nutrients and do not abuse it with the use of improper supplements, drugs or alcohol. Finally, the most important you need to show respect by representing God during competition.

Respect is attentive and focused. When you value and accept every person, you begin to understand that each has something to teach you. "Where love focuses on giving to others, respect shows a willingness to receive from them. Respect acknowledges another person's ability or potential to contribute . . . If you have had the opportunity to work in many environments and you have worked for both types of people—those who have and those who have not shown you respect—you understand how motivational respect can be. And you also know that you are more easily influenced by people that treat you well."[1]

Respect is both encouraging and appreciative. You understand the value of both giving and receiving support. The true athlete and great teams demonstrate this concept of respect with both verbal and physical cues that they are listening and learning such as eye contact and a voice or body language that says, thanks for thinking that I am capable of getting better.

Rules of the Road

**The Commandments
Life is about learning to
love, God, and others.**

**Integrity
To know and do what is right**

**Respect
Treat others the way you
want them to be treated**

Stat Sheet

Fundamentals: Basic Skills

1. Treating others the way you want to be treated.
2. Respect is the baseline for living by a higher standard.
3. Respect is valuing the person or situation that stands before you.
4. Respect is social character in action as it is given and received in public.
5. Respect is the value you place on something.
6. Respect shapes how you see any activity in which you will participate.

7. Respect in the NAIA model of Live 5: tolerant, considerate, attentive, encouraging, and appreciative.
8. All of the following are traits or qualities of respect. Pick one and discuss how it is seen in your life?
   - Respect is the baseline for living by a higher standard.
   - Respect begins with tolerance.
   - You need to learn to respect for yourself.
   - You need to learn respect for others.
   - You need to respect property.
   - You need to show respect by representing God during competition.

Strength and Conditioning Training: Improving Your Shape

"Do nothing from selfishness or empty conceit, but with humility of mind let each of you regard one another as more important than himself" (Philippians 2:3).

There are four roles at an athletic event

You can be an Official
You can be a Spectator
You can be a Competitor
You can be a Coach

You must choose one!

Positive Fan Behavior

1. Make an athletic event enjoyable and fun by demonstrating *good* sportsmanship. An athletic event gives the public the most notice-able reference to the institution's playing.
    *   What is the impression you want others to have about *your institution* after watching your TEAMS play?

2. Always remember that officials are there to be in charge of the game, make subjective judgments, and enforce the rules of the game while controlling play.

3. Attending an athletic event *does not* allow a person the right to act, say, or do anything they want.
    *   Are the values you are express-ing your personal beliefs? Would you say, act, and/or do these things if you were sit-ting at a game by yourself?

What Fan Behavior Is Unacceptable

1. Demeaning behavior
    *   Lack of respect for players, coaches, officials, and other fans.
    *   Personal attacks on another individual.

2. Profane and Crude behavior
    *   Obscenities
    *   Sexual harassment

3. Over-involved behavior
    *   Trying to be too *involved* in the *game*
    *   The attention should be on the game and the participants, *not* on the fans or crowd!

4. Uneducated behavior
    *   Berating an official whose call is correct
    *   Trying to coach from the stands

Encourage your fans to cheer for your team, not against the opponent!

Bruce Brown when speaking to a group of student athletes during one of his Proactive Coaching presentation, related the following scenario:

As a student athlete that has been challenged to uphold standards of **GOLD PRIDE** where would you step in and stop the behavior described in this situation?

You are in a leadership position at your school. You are attending a home basket-ball game and sitting with fellow students. The visiting team has a player shooting a free throw directly in front of your student section when a student or students in your stands exhibit the following behaviors.

At what point would you stand up, walk over, and tell the students that their behavior is wrong.

1. Yelling while the player prepares to shoot
2. Stomping feet while the player pre-pares to shoot

3. Waving your hands to visually distract the shooter

4. Waving and varying the yelling to both visually and verbally distract the shooter

5. Yelling, "Miss it" right before the release of the shot

6. Adding the players name while chanting, "Miss it, Susie, miss it"

7. Chanting her name Susie, Susie, Susie

8. Getting more personal: "Susie, you can't shoot"; "Susie, you are 1 for 5"; "Susie, give it up."

9. More personal: "Susie, you are the worst shooter on your team."

10. More personal: "Susie, you are ugly."

11. More personal: "Susie, you have fat legs."

12. "Susie, nice butt."

13. "Susie, you are gay."

14. "Susie, _____ ethnic slur."

I would stop the unsportsmanlike behavior at number _____. Why?

Game Day: Performing with Excellence

Using the NAIA model for **LIVE 5** write a short paragraph on what **RESPECT** means to you at this time in your collegiate experience and hope you might make this core value part of your lifestyle?

Endnotes

[1] James Maxwell. *Becoming a Person of Influence*. Nashville: Thomas Nelson, 1997, 43.

Responsibility

You choose what happens to you. Are you doing the best to fully accept that responsibility?

Pastor Phillip De Courcy in his weekly devotional offers a great illustration what it means to be responsible.

Paul Powell tells the story of Beverly King, who at one point was the richest man in Graham, Texas. King's presence was large in Graham since he owned the hotel, was a big-time stockholder and director at the bank, not to mention other business interests. Yet for all his money and status, he seldom dressed or acted the part. He usually spent his week going about town in his work clothes distributing books of matches advertising the bank. Given his unpretentious demeanor, he was mistaken one day by a traveling salesman for the town loafer. The salesman was having car trouble and was told by the local garage owner that he would have to stay a night in the hotel while his car was being fixed. The salesman asked Beverly King, who happened to be about the garage that afternoon, if he would mind carrying his bags down to the hotel. Mr. King decided to play along for the fun of it. As they both moved toward the hotel, Mr. King in tow with a bag in each hand, the salesman said, "As I came into town, I noticed a big house built on the hill. It must have been four or five thousand square feet." Mr. King said, "Yes, I have seen it." The stranger continued, "That surprises me. I would not have thought anybody around here could afford a house like that. Do you know who owns it?" Mr. King replied, "Yes, it belongs to me." The salesman took a sec-ond look at Mr. King, and then said, "How in the world could you afford a house like that?" Mr. King replied, "By carrying my own bags."

To be responsible means "carrying your own bags"; it means to model behavior that is a product of your conscious choice based on your values, your purpose, and your vision. In making your choices you must guard against the influence of the culture of ease that is ever present in our society. Character is all about how conscientiously you perform within your relationships. You need to be aware and careful to fulfill your part (responsibilities) with the team because the choices you make affect how others may act. Your responsibility is to make the choices that move you from where you are to a path toward pursuing excellence that will lead to significance.

Responsibility means having the discipline to hold yourself accountable for your choices. It is the ability to choose your response. Student athletes should be accountable to themselves, their teams, coaches, institutions and their sport. This includes making decisions in the areas of role modeling, education, self-control, respect, rules, refraining from enhancing drug, conditioning, and personal conduct.

Accountability builds trust between teammates; when teams are accountable, promises are kept, obligations are fulfilled, and teammates are seen as trustworthy. When accountability is not present, these things occur: everyone is quick to blame others, everyone is quick to make excuses, and everyone hesitates to tackle their problems because they do not want any responsibility for themselves or team improvement.

Every team member needs to be responsible for themselves and other team members. You need to first understand the team purpose and goals and then to be responsible to help advance them. Thus, helping each other reach both individual and team goals.

Responsibility requires commitment and perseverance. Commitment is dedicating yourself to following up on your words with action even if it means unexpected sacrifice. Perseverance and positive attitude are a choice not a skill. How quickly do you recover from a mistake? Do you bring others down with your attitude? Do you love the attention of the arena more than the competitive challenges? Perseverance allows you to keep focused on the pursuit of what is best for you and your team.

A responsible teammate is one that is consistent and your teammates look to as an example. Being consistent in anything you do is very important. A responsible person displays consistency. Are you reliable in every situation, can you count on yourself? Do you show initiative and stay the course? Do you have good judgment and common sense? Do you practice self-discipline and keep your emotions under control? A teammate that is not consistent and reliable exhibits the following traits so your teammates can never be sure that they can count on you. You display lots of ups and downs, peaks and valleys; you have trouble seeing things through and you give up easily.

"Make a careful exploration of who you are and the work you have been given, and then sink yourself into that. Don't be impressed with yourself. Don't compare yourself with others. Each of you must take responsibility for doing the creative best you can with your own life." (Galatians 6:4–5 MSG)

Rules of the Road

**The Commandments
Life is about learning to
love, God, and others.**

**Integrity
To know and do what is right**

**Respect
Treat others the way you
want them to be treated**

**Responsibility
Embrace the role you play on the team**

Stat Sheet

Fundamentals: Basic Skills

1. Embrace the role you play on the team.
2. The social force that binds me to the group or team.
3. Responsibility means having the discipline to hold yourself accountable for your choices.
4. To be responsible means to model behavior that is a product of your conscious choice based on your values, your purpose, and your vision.
5. Responsibility in the NAIA model of Live 5: conscientious, accountable, helpful, persevering, and reliable.

6. All of the following are traits or qualities of responsibility. Pick one and discuss how it is seen in your life?

- Responsibility means having the discipline to hold yourself accountable for your choices.
- How does trust between teammates develop by holding them accountable?
- Responsibility requires commitment and perseverance
- A responsible teammate is one that is consistent and your teammates look to as an example.

Strength and Conditioning Training: Improving Your Shape

"But if anyone does not provide for his relatives, and especially for members of his household, he has denied the faith and is worse than an unbeliever" (1 Timothy 5:8).

The Wooden Bowl

The person who removes a mountain begins by carrying away small stones.

I will guarantee you will remember the tale of the Wooden Bowl, tomorrow, a week from now, a month from now, a year from now

A frail old man went to live with his son, daughter-in-law, and a four-year-old grandson.

The old man's hands trembled, his eyesight was blurred, and his step faltered.

The family ate together at the table. But the elderly grandfather's shaky hand and failing sight made eating difficult. Peas rolled of his spoon onto the floor.

When he grasped the glass, milk spilled on the tablecloth. The son and daughter-in-law became irritated with the mess.

"We must do something about father," said the son.

"I've had enough of his spilled milk, noisy eating, and food on the floor"

So the husband and wife set a small table in the corner. There, Grandfather ate alone while the rest of the family enjoyed dinner.

Since Grandfather had broken a dish or two, his food was served in a wooden bowl.

When the family glanced in Grandfather's direction, sometimes he had a tear in his eye as he sat alone.

Still, the only words the couple had for him were sharp admonitions when he dropped a fork or spilled food.

The four-year-old watched in silence.

One evening before supper, the father noticed his son playing with wood scraps on the floor.

He asked the child sweetly, "What are you making?"

Just as sweetly, the boy responded, "Oh, I am making a little wooden bowl for you and Mama to eat your food when I grow up.

The four-year-old smiled and went back to work. The words so struck the parents so that they were speechless.

The tears started to stream down their cheeks. Though no word was spoken, both knew what must be done.

That evening, the husband took Grandfather's hand and gently led him back to the family table.

For the remainder of his days, he ate every meal with the family. And for some reason, neither the husband nor wife seemed to care any longer when a fork was dropped, milk spilled, or the tablecloth soiled.

On a positive note, I have learned that no matter what happens, how bad it seems today, life goes on, and it will be better tomorrow.

I have learned that you can tell a lot about a person by the way he/she handles four things: a rainy day, the elderly, lost luggage, and tangled Christmas tree lights.

I have learned that making a "living is not the same thing as making a life."

I have learned that life sometimes give you a second chance.

I have learned that you should not go through life with a catcher's mitt on both hands. You need to be able to throw something back sometimes.

I have learned that if you pursue happiness, it will elude you. But, if you focus on your family, your friends, the needs of others, your work and doing the very best you can, happiness will find you.

I have learned that whenever I decide something with an open heart, I usually make the right decision.

I have learned that even when I have pains, I do not have to be one.

I have learned that every day, you should reach out and touch someone. People love that human touch.

I have learned that I still have a lot to learn. I have learned that you should pass this on to everyone you care about.

1. **Is there some area in your life, with your team or with your family where you need to become more responsible? What is that and how can you be more responsible?**

Game Day: Performing with Excellence

Using the NAIA model for **LIVE 5** write a short paragraph on what *responsibility* means to you at this time in your collegiate experience and how you might intentionally make this core value part of your lifestyle.

Sportsmanship

Sportsmanship it is what makes good athletes great!

The characteristics that define sportsmanship demonstrate the interrelatedness of the ripple effect. The core value of sportsmanship is a microcosm of the ripple effect. It is a combination and reflection of the core values as well as the five *P*s. Perception, passion, potential, priorities, and the power of Christ provide you with a focus to pursue excellence and help you define and establish your identity. However, your identity needs to be channeled properly in being able to respond appropriately through the core value of sportsmanship. Sportsmanship is adhering to the highest principles of the core values of integrity, internal traits that guide behavior; respect, the baseline for living by a higher standard, and responsibility, being accountable to your values and convictions.

While the term *sportsmanship* is most frequently referred to as an athletic term, it definitely has meaning in every area of your life. The implementation of sportsmanship is actually putting the components of the ripple effect into action on a daily basis. Throughout your life you will be faced with situations both in and out of athletics that will require you to respond as a person of character.

How you respond through the example of sportsmanship determines the depth of your character. A tube of toothpaste provides a great example of this concept. When you squeeze a tube of toothpaste the paste comes out. When you are tested or squeezed, when pressure (temptation) comes you allow what is inside to come out (character). Will this be a bad reflection of you or will your character allow you to respond appropriately? Do you have the qualities of discipline detailed during the discussion in potential to respond in a positive manner in an athletic contest or when you are confronted with adversity; do you have the ability to do the right thing despite the cost and risks, to do it without any expectation of approval or advantage, but simply because it is the right thing to do?

Sportsmanship is being able to adhere to societal rules and regulation even if those guidelines differ somewhat with your current state of mind; it is the act of having poise and demonstrating Christ-like behavior no matter what the outcome of a game. Sportsmanship is the act of addressing your opponent and wishing them good luck. Sportsmanship is having the frame of mind and heart that seeks mutual benefit in your relationships with others; it is having the right value system and being able to express those values in stressful situations. Sportsmanship is acknowledging your coach at the end of the game even if he has been critical of your performance during the game because you respect the fact that he is just attempting to make you better; it is understanding how to add value to your life through consistent behavior that models your principles. Sportsmanship is the act of telling your opponent good game no matter how much pushing and shoving occurs during the contest. Sportsmanship is following and respecting the rules and regulations of the game and accepting the decisions of the official or umpire even though their calls went against you; it is following and accepting the rules and regulations of the organization you are a part of because you belong to that organization. Sportsmanship is being a person of honor who is accountable. Sportsmanship is the act of encouraging yourself after a tough loss no matter how poorly you played and after a victory acknowledging your strengths without taking advantage and to do so without boasting—that is sportsmanship.

The American dream fosters the concept of competition. The thought process is that if you worked hard enough and long enough you can achieve anything in life that you want. Competition formulated in the correct manner allows you to reach your true potential. It perpetuates the thought to be the best you are capable of becoming instead of doing whatever it takes to get ahead and win. The relationship among opponents should be built upon respect for each other, the game, the rules, and the honor of competition. In athletics, as in life, a reason to play the games is to have a winner and a loser. The reason we sponsor competition is to have a result. However, the most important element for those that participate in the competition is to win with honor, lose with dignity, and compete with character. This is the essences of sportsmanship in the athletic arena.

Most athletes will accept the rules of competition of the game because they have participated in the game all of their lives. However, many do not always value societal rules (laws) or regulations. Just as you will be a part of team all of your life, you will also have to adhere to a set of rules or standards outside of the rules of the game. In our society, we have rights and we have rules. Many of the social inequities that occur today are a result of people feeling their rights are being inhibited by the established rules. Throughout your life, you will be asked to do things that you believe are an infringement on your personal rights. Demonstrating sportsmanship in daily life is as paramount as that in the athletic arena. Again, it defines the depth of your character.

Rules are defined as a prescribed guide for conduct or action; an accepted procedure, custom, or habit; a regulating principle that is used as a basis for judgment such as morals, ethics, habits, established by authority, custom, or an individual as acceptable practices or principles.

Rights are defined as qualities (as adherence to duty or obedience to lawful authority) that together constitute the ideal of moral propriety or merit moral approval or something to which one has a just claim; the power or privilege to which one is justly entitled (voting rights, a person's right to decide or make a choice or a person's right to their opinion). A person has the right to be passionate about something and to pursue that passion.

There are two choices that a person has toward rules if they believe that their rights are being violated: (1) resist or rebel, or (2) respond.

Resistance is defined as the act or power of resisting, opposing, or withstanding. Rebellion means being opposed to one in authority or resistance to an established set of rules. No one likes to be told what they must do. Stubbornness and entitlement are the two most common behaviors that result when you resist or rebel. Both surface in your behavior as a result of self-centeredness. There is internal focus instead of external. The result is what can be termed "bad pride" and it is being fueled by your ego.

Stubbornness is defined as being unreasonably, often perversely unyielding or bullheaded; difficult to deal with. Proverbs 16:18 says, "First pride, then the crash, the bigger the ego, the harder the fall."

"Stubbornness is first cousin to arrogance, and pride always precedes a fall. When we think that we know it all . . . when we refuse to try another way of doing things . . . when we are determined to remain inflexible and ignorant, we are doomed to failure."[1] When you display stubbornness you dig in your heels. When you apply the brakes to stop a car you push down on the brake by digging in your heal and applying the break. The result is you stop your progress. You get further away from where you want to be (reaching your potential). You lose the focus of your vision and you see yourself as a victim. In this state you become closed minded and no longer have a teachable spirit. In Proverbs 13:10 it states, "Where there is strife, there is pride, but wisdom is found in those who take advice." You look inward instead of outward and the result is discouragement because there is no forward progress. Recovery time is reduced due to your mental approach so the discouragement last longer. You have trouble seeing things through and you allow disappointments that happened yesterday to interfere with today. On teams where stubbornness exists there is drama, moodiness and pouting.

The second most common behavior that occurs when there is resistance or rebellion is entitlement.

In 2 Corinthians 12:20, it states, "For I am afraid that when I come I may not find you as I want you to be, and you may not find me as you want me to be. I fear that there may be discord, jealousy, fits of rage, selfish ambition, slander, gossip, arrogance and disorder." The single biggest treat to any team's success is bad pride. This is a false pride and it says with words and actions "look at me I need attention." When these people win the pride that develops is self-oriented and egotistical; it comes and goes with winning and losing, it is attached to the outcome of games. There is arrogance, a sense of entitlement; you need to treat me special because I am an athlete. Normal rules do not apply to me because I was born tall or fast. On teams where entitlement exists there is an environment of manipulation and relationships are non-trusting.

The sportsmanship core value is a matter of being good (character) and doing right (actions) while participating in athletics and life. Sportsmanship implies fairness and equity in relationships, being grateful about your differences, sharing your disappointments, trusting God with your feelings, being courageous and take the initiative, being considerate of other's needs, being constructive with your words, being candid about problems, being confidential with information, being committed to your relationships. Learning how to be proactive in your relationships, make small commitments and keep them, being a light not a judge, being a model not a critic, being part of the solution not part of the problem, not arguing for other people's weaknesses, not arguing for your own weaknesses.

Many of the problems in dealing with the belief that your rights are being violated when it comes to rules and regulations can be contributed to the fact that we live in a culture today that promotes comfort and allows us to deviate from purpose without consequences. Two factors that define any activity are urgent and/or important. What you believe to be urgent matters press on you; you believe you need to act on these immediately. Urgent matters often are popular with others (your peers) and usually come from your environment. Important matters generally have more valuable because these matters contribute to your mission, values, and purpose. Important matters have to do with results. You generally react in urgent matters but respond to important matters. If you do not have a clear understanding of what is important for you in your life you are easily diverted into reacting to the urgent. You want for things now (instant gratification, free from the consequences of your choices), and you want things to be as easy as possible. You are willing to risk the important (pursuing excellence) for short-term urgency (violation of team or institutional rules) and hope that you will not be held accountable for your choice or actions. When you are in this mind set you are not unique or alone. This is a dilemma that many people face every day and because of this we have established four triggers that you can utilize to help you avoid risking the important and adhere to your values and make positive choices. To have your actions meet your principles instead of changing your principles to meet you action.

The following triggers provide a ripple effect within the core value of sportsmanship and incorporate the core values of integrity, respect, and responsibility. The triggers are predicated on this concept, "It is only important when it is important (OIWI)." Think about this statement. When is something important? In the academic area invariably at the beginning of the semester the professor hands out a syllabus for the class with all the assignments and due dates. When do those assignments become important to you that are due the last week of the class? Is it important in the first week, the fourth; no, most likely it becomes important toward the end and for most of us at the twelfth hour just before it is due. Another example is in the summer when you are supposed to work on your conditioning to report back to school in shape for your sport. We tend to procrastinate here also. The conditioning becomes important when you are not in the proper condition and you struggle during the first week of training. When you have to make a choice about importance you need to apply the following four triggers to help you avoid risking the important, help you adhere to your values and make positive choices.

The triggers are (1) planned abandonment, this is the proactive trigger (2) what is important now (WIN), this is the focus trigger, (3) win the event (WTE), this is the completion or finishing trigger, and get it done (GID), this is the fulfillment trigger. Planned abandonment is merely the practice of determining in advance what you will do in short-term urgency situations that are merely a distraction from your purpose. An athletic example of this might be how you want to respond to what you perceive to be a "bad" call from an umpire or an official. Another example is to predetermine how you will respond when confronted by your peers to do something that might be outside the rules and regulations on your team. Planned abandonment is integrity in action, you determine in advance that your yes means yes and your no means no.

What is important now (WIN) is a trigger that is extremely valuable in pressure or stressful situations to help you remain focused on the task at hand; the acronym of WIN relates well in the athletic arena. It makes you focus on what is important now; in a contest when you make a mistake, to focus on that mistake does not help you or your team, you must move on to what is important now, the next play. Outside the athletic arena, what is important now is valuable in making choices about not letting your teammates down. When in a situation that you deem questionable in terms of violating a rule or regulation, what is important now is how will the decision you are about to make going to affect my team and teammates. If the decision will not enhance you, your team, and your teammates, then what is important now is to not do it. Respect shapes the value you place on an activity, the baseline for living by a higher standard.

To win the event (WTE) works in conjunction with the concept of putting your personal signature on everything you do. When you sign something you want to make sure that your signature stands for something. The same is true for winning the event. When you do something you want to make sure that you do not just go through the motions; you want to give it your best effort. You want to win each event you take part in whether it is an athletic contest, a final test, or just developing a relationship. 1 Corinthians 9:25–27 (MSG) sums up the essence of winning the event, "You have all been to the stadium and seen the athlete's race. Everyone runs; one wins. Run to win. All good athletes train hard. They do it for a gold medal that tarnishes and fades. You are after one that is gold eternally. I do not know about you, but I'm running hard for the finish line. I'm giving it everything I've got. No sloppy living for me! I'm staying alert and in top condition. I'm not going to get caught napping, telling everyone else all about it and then missing out myself." Winning the event is staying accountable to your values and convictions as a responsible person.

Finally, get it done (GID) is the fulfillment trigger. Through this process of importance, you no longer a need to justify your behavior because you are staying true to your values. You learn to think inside yourself to find the solution for substantial insight toward your purpose. Fulfillment is beyond success and knowing that allows you to determine what roads and what action to take and the correct choices and decisions to make.

Discipline is paramount in the development of sportsmanship. Discipline is an attempt to establish a standard that modifies behavior. The values that come when an athlete embraces discipline are focused attention and effort. When discipline is balanced with love it is involved in every success. Real athletes see the bigger picture when it comes to discipline they realizes that the sacrifice of discipline needs to be made, not only do they accepts discipline they embrace it for the benefit of the team. The benefits of discipline that are involved with sportsmanship are attentiveness, you choose to be completely focused and attentive; enthusiasm, coming to practice with your motor running; sportsmanship; doing what is right for your team; responding to situations rather than react; developing patience; being a role model; respecting authority (parents, coaches, captains, officials, adults); accepting personal responsibility being able to make the right choices when you are away from the team; believing in yourself—are you trustworthy; honesty—do you deal with the truth; habit the ability to do it every time.

Discipline involves learning to respect the game, respect for your teammates, respect for your coach, and respect for yourself.

Discipline sets the athlete apart and gives them an edge.

What occurs when an athlete rejects discipline? Discipline is like a dirty word; you view discipline as a punishment, which results in feeling sorry for yourself and thus, feel like you need to resist discipline; this resistance is displayed in anger—temper. It is important not to confuse anger and frustration with being competitive because anger and frustration are wasted energy. Visible anger discourages your teammates and encourages your opponents and does not give you any competitive edge at all. Emotion is great when used in a positive way, but temper is emotion out of control that damages you as an individual and your team.

Great competitors can focus and channel their emotion in ways that helps their own performance as well. Discipline is a choice it is not a skill. Do you accept and embrace discipline for the betterment of yourself and the team? Do you resist it? "Lack of ability can be forgiven but you cannot ever forgive lack of discipline" (Forrest Gregg, a member of the Pro Football Hall of Fame).

Other traits that are enhanced through sportsmanship are the following: obedience, fulfilling instructions and rules; fairness, looking at a decision from multiple viewpoints; justice, taking personal responsibility to uphold what is pure, right, and true; hospitality, sharing cheerfully with those whom I come in contact. Humility, seeing the contrast between what is perfect and where I am at.

Nicole Bataclan, "In the spirit of sportsmanship."

Only a Champion

Day in, day out on the mind
All comes down to competition
Result of years of preparation.
In those seconds of restlessness
When the body can take no more
Dream of a medal reassure.
Will to succeed is eminent
Breathes through each atom and cell
To have what only a champion can smell.
In the spirit of sportsmanship
Fair play is to be endeavored
The performance to be savored.
Now is everything you pursued
Aspiring in the end
To proudly sing the national anthem.
A steep climb to that podium
Be the best that you can be
And have what only a winner can see.

Sportsmanship it is what makes good athletes great!

Rules of the Road

The Commandments
Life is about learning to love, God and others.

Integrity
To know and do what is right

Respect
Treat others the way you want them to be treated

Responsibility
Embrace the role you play on the team

Sportsmanship
Bring your best to all competition

Stat Sheet

Fundamentals: Basic Skills

1. Bring your best to all competition.
2. Is following the rules, spirit, and etiquette of athletic competition as well as those regulations that govern other areas of your life.
3. The characteristics that define sportsmanship demonstrate the interrelatedness of the ripple effect.
4. How you respond through the example of sportsmanship determines the depth of your character.
5. Discipline is paramount in the development of sportsmanship.

6. Sportsmanship in the NAIA model of Live 5: cooperative, fair, gracious, honorable, and humble.
7. **Sportsmanship is being able to adhere to societal rules and regulation even if those guidelines differ somewhat with your current state of mind. In the examples listed below dealing with sportsmanship put an "S" next to the ones that would be a strength and an "I" next to the ones you would need improvement in your life. Then take one strength and a one improvement and discuss why?**

_____ It is the act of having poise and demonstrating Christ-like behavior no matter what the outcome of a game.

_____ Sportsmanship is the act of addressing your opponent and wishing them good luck.

_____ Sportsmanship is having the frame of mind and heart that seeks mutual benefit in your relationships with others.

_____ It is having the right value system and being able to express those values in stressful situations.

_____ Sportsmanship is acknowledging your coach at the end of the game even if he has been critical of your performance during the game because you respect the fact that he is just attempting to make you better.

_____ It is understanding how to add value to your life through consistent behavior that models your principles; sportsmanship is the act of telling your opponent good game no matter how much pushing and shoving occurs during the contest.

_____ Sportsmanship is following and respecting the rules and regulations of the game and accepting the decisions of the official or umpire even though their calls went against you.

_____ It is following and accepting the rules and regulations of the organization you are a part of because you belong to that organization.

_____ Sportsmanship is being a person of honor who is accountable.

_____ Sportsmanship is the act of encouraging yourself after a tough loss no matter how poorly you played and after a victory acknowledging your strengths without taking advantage and to do

so without boasting, that is sportsmanship.

Strength and Conditioning Training: Improving Your Shape

"Do nothing from rivalry or conceit, but in humility count others more significant than yourselves" (Philippians 2:3).

Nine Reasons I Swear

It pleases my Mom so much
It is a display of my character
It proves I have great self-control
It indicates how clearly my mind functions
It makes conversation so pleasant
It leaves no doubt in anyone's mind as to my upbringing
It impresses people
It makes me a very desirable personality to those around me
It is an unmistakable sign of my culture and refinement

Swearing is merely the easiest example of undisciplined communication.

Discuss the concept in terms of "it is only important" and how that might relate to you. Where are you with your words and actions.

Game Day: Performing with Excellence

Using the NAIA model for **LIVE 5** of **SPORTSMANSHIP** relate how you can apply the four triggers mention in this section to improve your ability to make choices.

1. Planned abandonment
2. What is important now (WIN)
3. Win the event (WTE)
4. Get it done (GID)

Endnotes

[1.] Laurie Beth Jones. *Jesus CEO, Using Ancient Wisdom for Visionary Leadership*. New York: Hyperion, 1992, 5.

Servant Leadership

Whoever wants to be great must become a servant
—Mark 10:43

"You were put on earth to make a contribution. You were not created just to consume resources—to eat, breathe, and take up space. God designed you to make a difference with your life. While many best-selling books offer advice on how to 'get' the most out of life, that is not the reason God made you. You were created to add to life on earth, not just to take from it. God wants you to give something back . . . it is called your 'ministry' or service. You are not saved by service but you are saved for service. In God's kingdom, you have a place, a purpose, a role, and a function to fulfill. This gives your life great significance and value."[1]

If being a servant leader is the pathway to real significance you need to decide how you will serve. In Jesus's ministry, He asked the question, "What do you want me to do for you?" He is asking you that same question. Jesus defines the importance of servanthood in addition to providing an example of the importance of serving or being a servant leader. Mahatma Gandhi said, "The best way to find yourself is to lose yourself in the service of others."

Being a servant is not about position, status, power, or skill. It is about your approach to life and your attitude toward others. The concept of servant leadership starts by being a servant first. A servant leader must first learn to serve before taking on a leadership position. Servant leaders must focus on the well-being and individual growth of others.

Servanthood embodies many qualities the first of which is the ability to become selfless. A selfless person is one who is more concerned about the happiness and well-being of another than about his or her own convenience or comfort, one who is willing to serve another when it is neither sought for nor appreciated, or one who is willing to serve even those whom he or she dislikes. A selfless person displays a willingness to sacrifice, a willingness to put aside personal wants, and needs, and feelings.

In the athletic arena, simply put selflessness is putting the needs of the team ahead of yours in every decision (both on and off the court). This is where we get the statement, "Do not do anything to let your teammates down." In your family or with other relationships outside the athletic arena, servanthood is the same but might be stated differently as the ability to put others ahead of yourself and your personal desires. This concept is not easily accomplished because all of us as humans are selfish. Being selfless is the action step for putting the "three Es" (empathy, excellence, and emulate) into practice. Simone De Beauvoir once said, "One's life has value as long as one attributes value to the life of others, by means of love, friendship, indignation and compassion."

"How we treat others is really a reflection of how we think about ourselves." Philosopher-poet Eric Hoffner captured that thought:

"The remarkable thing is that we really love our neighbor as ourselves; we do unto others as we do unto ourselves. We hate others when we hate ourselves. We are tolerant toward others when we tolerate ourselves. We forgive others when we forgive ourselves. It is not love of self but hatred of self which is the root of the troubles that afflict our world.'"[2]

Servanthood requires you to have the confidence in yourself that will provide you the security to reach out to others. Most people will help someone if they are compelled to do so. In other words, they will serve if there is a crisis or they have to. Many times when you are hesitant to serve because you are wondering what others might be thinking about you, remember this, most of the time, other people are not thinking about you because they are thinking about themselves. In servanthood, you need to be able to learn to look beyond yourself. Service to others needs to be an act of the heart. If you serve from the heart, your insecurity will be reduced and will gain confidence in yourself to be able to walk across the room to serve someone. Mary McLeod Bethune once said, "Faith is the first factor in life devoted to service. Without it, nothing is possible. With it, nothing is impossible." Mahatma Gandhi said, "Service which is rendered without joy helps neither the servant nor the served. But all other pleasures and possessions pale into nothingness before service which is rendered in a spirit of joy." Remember, life is not measured on how many breaths you take but how many moments take your breath away.

To fully comprehend having a servant's heart and the ability to be a servant leader you need an understanding of the lack of selflessness, selfishness. Again, we can all relate to selfishness because we have lived most of our life being selfish. Selfishness looks to satisfy your own need first (selfish with effort, selfish with attention, selfish with immature behavior); selfish people are absorbed in their own performance, quick to criticize teammates, they love to coast and avoid hard workouts and avoid daily responsibilities; you will never see a great team where the most talented players are not the best and hardest workers, the best listeners or willing to do what it takes to make the team better; the strength of the team is going to always be impacted by the weakest link and weakest attitude no matter how we try to cover it up or rationalize it, compensate for it the poorest attitude will come to light and especially if it involves a talented player and disrupt the function of the team.

Selfish athletes take short cuts because they are selfish with their effort and attention. We have a term for these people; we call them selective participants. This is a player who is physically talented and selfish with their effort or attention has chosen to be a selective participant. Traits of a selective participant are they choose when they will work and when they will coast; they choose when they will focus, when they will tune out; they choose when they show respect to the coach, they choose when they do not; they are quick to criticize teammates, quick to excuse themselves; they are the last in line, blame others for mistakes; they take shortcuts, like easy practices and days off, want to save it for the game; they live by their own agenda, are absorbed in their own performance; they choose when they will be a good teammate, they choose when they are not; all that matters to them is what they get out of the game for themselves; selective participants are team killers, energy sappers but they cannot hide.

A selfless person demonstrates enthusiasm—passion. The selfish person is too cool to show enthusiasm—passion. The selfless person puts their heart in their work every day. Coaches search for the heart of a team, because the person who has or is the heart can bring out the best in everybody else. Mike Krzyzewski said, "You had better understand that if you want people on your team who are fully committed, then you had better be fully committed to a course of action that allows proper use of that commitment. I have friends with whom I went to school who are buried at West Point cemetery. I will never forget that. So if I ask an eighteen year old on my team for his full commitment, I am going to make certain that whenever I am leading him, both the destination and the journey will be worthy."[3]

Being a servant leader that understands teamwork is a rare gift that allows ordinary people to attain extraordinary results. Being a part of a great team at least once in your athletic experience can influence who you are for the remainder of your life. William Arthur Lloyd once said, "We must be silent before we can listen. We must listen before we can learn. We must learn before we can prepare. We must prepare before we can serve. We must serve before we can lead." "Where is your heart when it comes to serving others?"[4]

Are you motivated by desire to help others? If you really want to become a servant leader, you have to decide about servanthood. "If your attitude is to be served rather than to serve, you may be headed for trouble. If this is an issue in your life, then heed this advice:

Stop lording over people, and start listening to them.
Stop role-playing for advancement, and start risking for other's benefit.
Stop seeking your own way, and start serving others."[5]

Being a leader who serves is very different from being a servant leader."
—Isabel O. Lopez

Rules of the Road

The Commandments
Life is about learning to love, God and others.

Integrity
To know and do what is right

Respect
Treat others the way you want them to be treated

Responsibility
Embrace the role you play on the team

Sportsmanship
Bring your best to all competition

Servant Leadership
Serve the common good of the team

Stat Sheet

Fundamentals: Basic Skills

1. Serving the greater good.
2. Servant-leadership encourages individuals to serve others while staying focused on achieving results in line with the team's values.
3. Being selfless.
4. Servant Leadership in the NAIA model of Live 5: empowering, visionary, interconnected, generous, and assertive.
5. **Define the term "selective participant"? Have you ever been a selective participant? When? Why?**

Strength and Conditioning Training: Improving Your Shape

"When He had washed their feet and put on His outer garments and resumed His place, He said to them, "Do you understand what I have done to you? You call me Teacher and Lord, and you are right, for so I am. If I then, your Lord and Teacher, have washed your feet, you also ought to wash one another's feet. For I have given you an example, that you also should do just as I have done to you" (John 13:12–15).

About seven years ago, Coach Wooden and I were in Boise, Idaho, speaking to a group of educators. I don't think they wanted to hear from me so much; they wanted to hear from Coach. How do I know? It's simple. When it came to the questions and answers segment, I had lots of answers, but nobody asked me a question. They put us up in a high-end hotel. You know, the kind where you get the "His and Hers Terry Cloth Bathrobes?"

The morning after, we were preparing to head to the airport to return home. I was already in the hotel lobby when Nan, Coach's daughter, asked if I would go up to Coach's room and help him bring his bags down. As I approached his room, I saw his door was propped open with his neatly-placed luggage. So I walked in.

The ninety-year-old "Coach of the Century" was washing out the coffee maker in the bathroom sink. He took out the coffee bag and placed it in the trash and then rinsed the dispenser until the water was clean. Then, he placed it carefully, upside-down, in the sink so it could drain.

Walking with a semi-shuffle because of his bad knees and slightly bent over, he next collected the trash from the other baskets in the room and consolidated them into the bathroom basket. Finally, he placed all the dirty towels on the bathroom sink.

When I looked at the bed, I saw Coach had stripped it, leaving a neat pile of sheets and pillow cases. Then he looked at me, smiled, and said, "Okay, Swen. I think we're ready to go now." Then, he walked back into the room, turned off the light next to the bed, walked out into the hall, and closed the door behind him.

When I was at UCLA, after we played a road game, Coach made sure we left the locker room as clean, or cleaner, than we found it. All towels were placed on a table in one pile and all trash was picked up and put in its proper place. I clearly remember three occasions when, before a home practice, Coach would read us a letter he had received from the custodian of a university we had competed with, expressing amazement and gratitude for our consideration.

Is it a coincidence, the most successful men's basketball college coach of all time has deep consideration for others and believes he is no better than anyone else, or is there a direct relationship between consideration and success? Just asking.

By the way, to this day, when I lodge somewhere overnight, I leave my room in the same condition Coach did, just in case he's got a spy reporting to him from Motel 6. I wouldn't put it past him.

1. As Gandhi said, "The best way to find yourself is to lose yourself in service of other." How are you serving others?

2. What would your relationships say is the driving force of your life? Is being selfless part of your character?

Game Day: Performing with Excellence

Using the NAIA model for **LIVE 5** write a short paragraph on what **SERVANT LEADERSHIP** means to you at this time in your collegiate experience and how you might intentionally make this core value part of your lifestyle.

Endnotes

[1]   Rick Warren. *What on Earth Am I Here For?* Zondervan: 2013, 225–226.
[2]   James Maxwell. *Becoming a Person of Influence.* Nashville: Thomas Nelson, 1997, 136–137.
[3]   Mike Krzyzewski. *Leading With the Heart.* Warner Books: 2001, 62.
[4]   James Maxwell. *Becoming a Person of Influence.* Nashville: Thomas Nelson, 1997, 138.
[5]   James Maxwell. *Becoming a Person of Influence.* Nashville: Thomas Nelson, 1997, 138.

Section IV

The Culture We Create Permeates Everything

We Touch

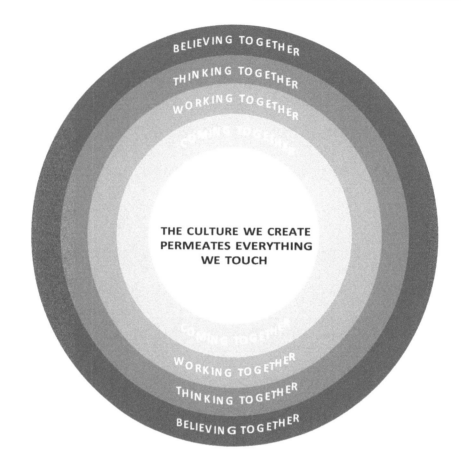

Establishing and Defining GOLD PRIDE

Establishing a culture that perpetuates tradition is a process.

The process is a series of actions or steps created to achieve an end (result). It is a process that establishes a culture that lives through succeeding generations. The culture created must underscore the mission, vision and values of the program. Great programs with established cultures are not great simply by chance, they are intentionally created.

Coming Together Is a Beginning

We want to create a culture where everyone believes GOLD PRIDE is theirs. It belongs to all of us and it is the responsibility of all of us to sustain it and to defend its values, purely because it is OURS.

The collegiate student athletes of today will become the societal leaders of tomorrow; this is an awesome responsibility. Are you preparing yourself mentally, physically, emotionally, relationally, and spiritually for this task?

All student athletes want to excel in the sport of their passion. Being a student athlete offers many challenges on and off the field of play. One of the most important challenges is that every student athlete wants to fit in, in the campus environment, with their team, in the residence halls, with other students; they want to be accepted by their coach and teammates and they want to show that they belong. What most new student athletes do not recognize is that to be able to be a total fit they need to be able to be accepted for more than their athletic skill in a quality program; those that are in a quality program remain in the program because they bring balance to the program. They have demonstrated excellence competitively, in the classroom, in their character development, and in their spiritual formation.

Emphasizing the word "together" indicates that you want to be a part of something bigger than yourself. Coming together is about beginning to understand and become a part of a new culture. Coming together is about helping you to understand the vision of **GOLD PRIDE**. Tony Dungy in his book *The Mentor Leader* makes this statement, "The culture we create permeates everything we touch." **GOLD PRIDE** was intentionally developed for this reason. Defining what you are doing and what the vision is brings clarity. Knowing and understanding the vision creates common ground for team members. When the culture is built through *tradition*, team members take *ownership* of what they are doing and realize it is important and essential for a higher purpose allowing them to become part of something bigger than themselves.

Coming together includes being a part of your team to develop your skills and talents in your sport but it includes a great deal more. It is about you not only improving athletically, but a commitment to your academic progress, your character development and your spiritual formation. In addition,

it is recognition that your sports program is special but that you also have a commitment to the entire athletic program. Your teammates include more than those on your individual team, they include all the athletic staff and student athletes on all the other teams. The whole group becomes your **GOLD PRIDE** team.

For anyone to move forward in anything, life, athletics, writing a term paper, or deciding on an academic major, they need direction.

If you do not have direction then you are allowing yourself to drift. Therefore, as a collegiate student athlete, you need to develop direction of who you want to be or where you want to go. Each part of your life—today's behavior, tomorrow's behavior, next week's behavior, next month's behavior—can be examined in the context of what really matters most to you. You need to make decisions that will enhance your destiny.

Many times over the years, I have heard this comment from alumni student athletes that have graduated and returned to campus, "I wish I would have listened, understood and applied what I was told in college because it would have made things easier for me." In other words, I wish I knew then, when I was a student athlete, what I know now.

As a student athlete, you have the capacity and ability to establish yourself but might not have the maturity to do so. Proverbs 13:16 offers valuable advice related to your collegiate experience, "Every prudent man acts out of knowledge." Maturity is having a realistic view of yourself, knowing your shape. Part of coming together in **GOLD**

PRIDE is the understanding the core covenants of empathy, excellence, and emulate as the cornerstones of **GOLD PRIDE**. The interlocking circles exhibit the core covenants that **GOLD PRIDE** embraces and they need to become part of your core.

Empathy is the building block for successful relationships. The single most important principle in developing empathy is the principle of seeking first to understand then to be understood. Empathy means to understand another person's feelings, thoughts, and desires. Empathy is the ability to see with the eyes of another, listen with the ears of another, and feel with the heart of another.

Empathy is a selfless act that enables you to learn more about people and relationships with people. Empathy is the foundation upon which morality is built. Empathy is real; it allows a person to feel wanted, understood and accepted for their authentic self. Humility is a value that enhances your ability to be more empathetic. It enables you to pay attention to those in your inner circle, to their feelings and expressions. Be cognizant about how they might be feeling.

Try to avoid labeling your teammate's emotions and behaviors. Being aware of your teammate's behaviors, thoughts, actions, and responses will help you be more empathetic and help them with their needs.

A teachable spirit is a value that contributes to a person developing empathy. What is your teachable spirit, are you coachable; are you open to the concepts presented by *The Ripple Effect* and investing in them to become more than you have become? Many times it is difficult to recognize that just because you believe something does not mean that it is correct or that you are right. Pausing to reflect and analyze your own beliefs, thoughts, and prejudices and learn to see the other view is part of having a teachable spirit and being more empathetic. Search for things that you share in common with someone who you at first did not understand and use that commonality to begin to develop a connection with that person.

Being an effective communicator is paramount to being more empathetic. Understanding is the desired outcome or goal in any communication process. Listening is one of the most important ways you can show empathy, and this means truly listening. When you listen to someone, you are giving that person your undivided attention; you are engaged in what they is saying. True listening means being present. Establish eye contact and face them. Listening requires three things. First, it reflects to them that you understand what the content of what they said. Second, it reflects your emotional reaction. Reflecting your emotions is a key part of empathy because it helps the person better understand and helps them to regulate their own emotions. Their reaction also helps you regulate your response. Third, your response provides them with an indication of expected behavior. Expressing your behavior is a key element, because again you are demonstrating that you understand their emotional state and helping them figure out a behavior to move forward with.

Just listening to a teammate is not going to provide a connection between the two of you. To deepen your relationship with a teammate requires you to become vulnerable with them. Opening up emotionally is difficult at times but it shows your teammate that you are real and willing to be trusted. Empathy is a two-way street. It is about sharing vulnerabilities and emotional connection, so to truly practice empathy, you have to share your own inner desires, thoughts and faults. To practice empathy, you have to be open to the possibility and the opportunity of opening up, especially those in the inner circle of the team.

Being available to your teammates and offering help is a great act of empathy because it demonstrates you are willing to sacrifice your time and effort to do something for them without asking anything in return. Offering help can be a simple act. Just offering the opportunity to help can be an empathetic gesture. Telling a teammate that if they need anything they can ask, opening up the way for providing help and support. Be positive in your words. Speak with a purpose; be responsible for honest and direct communication focusing on being truthful and speaking with integrity.

Words are powerful. The importance of words; what you say to others—and to yourself—can have a huge impact. Speaking with good purpose is about always considering the intention of our words. Your mouth directs where you go. Words lead you; words direct where you are going to go like the rudder of a boat. Your words can destroy what you have; they are like fire—fire can be good and warm you up or fire can be like a brush fire and destroy everything in sight. Your words displays who you really are; like spring water at a well; water can be refreshing or it can be poisonous; what is in your heart leaks out in your words. Words have the power to uplift and enlighten or put down and depress. A few cutting words spoken in a moment of anger can affect us for a long time, perhaps even a lifetime. On the other hand, a few kind words can make a very positive difference . . . sometimes for a lifetime. When you do respond you need to do so with honest, careful, and building or encouraging words. It is more important to speak the truth in love as opposed to being brutally honest. Honesty comes from the heart. You cannot treat communication as a battle between you and the person or teammate you are conversing with. The first step is awareness. Think before you speak. Make sure your intention is positive and your words are sincere. If you always think before you speak instead of just blurting out whatever comes to mind, you can learn to consider the reason for your words and make sure you are speaking with good purpose; will your words build someone up or put them down?

Sometimes you will have negative thoughts, but you do not have to say everything you think. In other words think before you speak:

T: Is it truthful?
H: Is it helpful (does it build up or harm)?
I : Is it inspirational?
N: Is it necessary?
K: Is it kind?

There will be times when you need to share critical thoughts. At these times, if your purpose and how you phrase your words is considered first, sharing honest and direct feedback can be very positive and powerful, and build trust. Speaking with good purpose is the cornerstone of healthy relationships. If you were given $100 for every time you use a word to build someone up and a $100 were taken away from you every time you used a harmful word toward someone where would your account be?

When mutual trust exists in communication between teammates, they will to go out of their way to help and support each other. Trust is the emotional bank account between two people that enables them to have a win-win performance agreement. This is a metaphor that describes the amount of trust a person has built in a relationship. Deposits build and repair trust in relationships. Withdrawals lessen or destroy trust in relationships. Depending on the size one withdrawal can destroy an account's balance.

Deposits include the following: clear expectations, kindness, courtesy, making and keeping promises, loyalty to the absent, ability to apologize, and seeking first to understand. *Extraordinary deposits* include exercising patience with others, distinguish-

ing between the person and the behavior or performance of that person; assuming the best of others; admitting your mistakes, apologizing, and asking forgiveness; renewing your commitment to things you have in common; being open to the influence of others; accepting the person and the situation; agreeing on the limits, rules, expectations, and consequences; being there for others and letting natural consequences teach responsible behavior.

Withdrawals on the other hand are created when the following behavior occurs: manipulation; thinking win-lose or lose-win; being defensive; not recognizing or rewarding good performance; being dishonest; displaying favoritism; sending mixed messages; showing a lack of courage or consideration or taking advantage of others.

If two people trust each other, based on the trustworthiness of each other, they can then enjoy clear communication, empathy, synergy, and productive interdependency.

Enriching the emotional bank account allows teammates to grow closer and helps you develop empathy together. Actions that enhance the emotional bank account include: remembering every interaction is an opportunity to open an account; you never close an account; making genuine deposits; being consistent in your actions and responses; giving your most constant deposit to your closest relationships; making sure the deposit is a deposit in the recipient's eye; discern what to overlook; commit to no withdrawals and challenge your biases and assumptions.

A lot of assumptions and prejudices are based on erroneous information. Being able to withhold judgment can be difficult at times when you first meet or interact with someone. Everybody sees the world differently based on their own experiences, their home environment, their culture, and their religious convictions. In order to show empathy to a teammate you need to understand their perspective and what that perspective is based on. Most people find it easier to be empathetic to people they have a connection with or have shared common experiences. An empathetic person attempts to gain a deeper understanding of their perspective without making a value judgment. This does not necessarily mean that their view is correct, but taking the time to gain a deeper perspective will help you be more empathetic towards them. However, this is not to say that if someone is acting in a reprehensible manner that you should not intervene or say something. Speaking up is an act of courage and compassion.

Ten reasons why you should explicitly work to enhance your ability to empathize with your teammates?

1. You will better understand the needs of your teammates.
2. You will be more likely to treat your teammates you care about the way you wish they would treat you.
3. You will more clearly understand the perception you create in your teammates with your words and actions.
4. You will have less trouble dealing with interpersonal conflict.
5. You will be able to more accurately predict the actions and reactions of your teammates.
6. You will learn how to better motivate your teammates.
7. You will more effectively convince your teammates of your point of view.
8. You will enhance your ability to communicate your perspective but understand the perspectives of your teammates.
9. You will find it easier to deal with the negativity of your teammates if you can better understand their motivations and fears to be able to accept the situation for what it is.
10. You will be a better leader, a better follower, and most important, a better teammate.

Excellence is your ability to focus on and demonstrate excellence in all the ways your life calls for. Aristotle wrote, "We are what we repeatedly do. Excellence then is not an act but a habit." Excellence begins with a ten word vocabulary:

1. One word: Please
2. Two words: Thank you
3. Three words: I love you
4. Four words: Can I help you?

Everything important starts with your investment in it. Basketball coach Mike Krzyzewski, emphasizes to those who are part of the Duke Basketball program, "Everything you do is important." You need to make the most of every opportunity. Concentrate on what you are doing while you are doing it. In displaying excellence no task is too small for you to execute to the best of your ability. You need to be disciplined enough to do the right thing, at the right time, as best as you can. Being excellent is about focusing on the present instead of the later, or next week, or next month, or next year.

You need to develop an attitude of excellence. You always will be confronted with distraction and opportunities to do something else, something other than what you are doing now. Do not wasting your time and energy on those other things; make what you are doing now "important" instead of focusing on things you would like to do, could have done, or should have done. Whenever your thoughts are occupied with something other than what you are doing, you miss the "importance" of the moment and the present opportunity slips away. Excellence becomes the ability to focus your attention on the present moment and the willingness to make whatever you are doing most important.

Excellence is not always about achieving or being successful. Feedback from failures provides the information you need to learn so you can succeed. Learn from your mistakes. To be excellent in your failures you may need to change the way you think about failure. Rather than viewing failure in a negative way where you put yourself down and think, you are a failure, think of failure as a valuable learning experience. When you look at your mistakes, see the mistakes as opportunities, and learn from them, rather than seeing the mistakes as a negative, begin to develop a habit that will eventually lead you to a greater degree of excellence.

You may be reluctant to try different things because you are afraid of failing. Fear of failure does nothing but keep you in your comfort zone where you stick with the familiar, the "safe" choices where you do not "risk" another failure. When you step out of our comfort zone—when you are willing to try something new—that is when you take a step toward success. The only real failure is not learning from your mistakes. Excellence allows you to look at what went wrong, change what you did, and try again by applying what you learned.

Excellence is exhibited when you are willing to take ownership and responsibility for the choices you make. When you take responsibility for your choices, others know they can count on you and you earn their respect. Excellence is demonstrated when you take responsibility for your actions, putting your personal signature on everything you do. Being responsible for your thoughts, feelings, words, and actions, owning the choices you make and the results that follow. When you take ownership of everything you do and say, and stop blaming things outside yourself for situations that occur in your life, you have greater control and are demonstrating excellence. You may not be able to control everything that happens in your life but you can control how you respond to what happens. Ownership is a life developing concept. You take ownership of your education, your relationships, your development, your social decision—all areas of your life. When this occurs, you become more confident and the habit of excellence in your life is enhanced.

Finally, flexibility is a quality of excellence. Flexibility is the willingness to try something different when you realize that what you are doing is not working. There will be times that you are faced with situations that are different from what you had originally planned; one way to deal with these situations is to be rigid and continue to do things in the same way over and over—another is to handle them with flexibility. Being flexible is responding to changing or new situations in ways that you move forward. Be willing to do things differently, to change what you are doing to achieve the outcome you desire. Flexibility allows you to choose the best option to accomplish the outcome. Flexibility is about not getting locked in to one way of doing something. Flexibility is about recognizing all kinds of habits or patterns or activities in your life that are not working and changing them, and even changing them again until you find the one that works.

Parable of talents in the Bible teaches us the importance of excellence by recognizing and using our God gifted talent and abilities (waste it, resist it, or invest in it). Three servants were given talents by the master; one was given one talent and he buried his in the ground for fear of losing it. One was given two talents and he invested it and returned twice as much; one was given five talents and he invested it and the return was also doubled. The moral of the story is that excellence is not measured by the number of talents you have but by what you do with the talents you are given. Are you aligning your priorities with your passion to maximize your potential? One person's excellence is different from another's.

It does not take great athletic ability to give an excellent effort. Values that contribute to a person developing excellence are: a work ethic; one of the most important life lessons that can be taken from sport is the ability to work; to finish what you start in every area of your life; ask for help when you do not understand; pay attention to detail; to have focused attention, focused effort, to listen and concentrate. Consistency to be reliable in every situation; can you count on yourself. Confidence that is always based on quality of preparation and is carried quietly; all great teams throughout history have had one thing in common, unity of purpose to be excellence. Everything important starts with your investment in it.

Develop an attitude of excellence.

Emulating the character qualities of Christ is the most difficult for most people. This is due to the fact that for most of us we have been dependent for most of our lifetime. We have not learned to be selfless and in fact are very selfish. To emulate Christ means serving others, the value of being selfless. Service to others is empathy and excellence put into acts and action. It means selflessly putting the best interest of others (the team) first. Selfless is becoming a servant leader. Servant-leadership encourages individuals to serve others while staying focused on achieving results in line with the team's values; being a part of something bigger than yourself by developing a great team. The process of becoming a team player is a decision based on attitude. Teamwork is a conscious step from dependence (me, me, me), to independence (me on my own), to interdependence (we or us). It is purposeful and it is intentional. It is real and it is felt. It is authentic and has passion. One rule: Do not let your teammates down. The sacrifice is simply this: setting aside your personal rights and goals for the benefit of the group (team). Being a servant leader that understands teamwork is a rare gift that allows ordinary people to attain extraordinary results. Being a part of a great team (legacy team or team of significance) at least once in your athletic experience can influence who you are for the remainder of your life.

A legacy team is defined as follows: a team that is formed intentionally; works to its potential; where there are no regrets; the life of the team lives on after the team is done competing; one rule of these teams, do not let your teammates down.

Some time ago, I came across the tool that can be used to help you in your ability to learn something new. This is particularly helpful to college-age students because they come from a variety of backgrounds, cultures and experiences. The tool has three phases: adopt, adapt, adept.

In adopting a thought, idea, or concept you adopt it at face value. You do not resist the change in thinking but merely are open to the potential of the thought. Adapting means that you make modifications in the thought you accepted at face value. You apply your own values, principles and standards to modify the original thought. Finally, you become adept at making the original thought part of your approach that fits you and your needs. In *The Ripple Effect*, "The Culture We Create Permeates Everything We Touch," we will use this tool. Working together adopt, thinking together adapt and believing together adept.

Having a vision and developing a lifestyle that incorporates the core covenants of the three *E*s helps keep things in perspective. It allows for a stable platform. It keeps your focus on the future not the past. The focus on the future keeps you motivated to achieve whatever is necessary for sustained success and to move toward significance. It keeps you focused on the pursuit of excellence, not the path of mediocrity. The pursuit of excellence forces you to confront your weaknesses, adapt your thinking, and keep your ego in check. We do not want to be just competitors on an athletic field but individuals striving to surpass other competitors by establishing a standard of competitive excellence based on values that we live by on the sidelines and on the sidewalks. These values allow you to hold each other accountable to the same standard of excellence. It helps you become the right kind of role model.

Defines who we are . . .

1. **It is about breaking the mold of what society believes is the image of a college-age student athlete.**
2. **It is about something GOD is doing in the hearts and minds of student athletes.**

3. **It is about an idea—it is about rebelling against low expectations, accepting existing standards as well as establishing and adhering to higher standards that allow each student athlete to attain Significance**

An atmosphere of communication and trust through empathy, excellence, and emulation help to establish tradition. Older team members will establish credibility with the newer ones. Even though they do not like everything about you, they will still say, "You are trustworthy, committed to us as a team,"[2] comments Mike Krzyzewski.

A few years ago Bruce Brown of Proactive Coaching used the definition of a tribe to describe a team:

A group of people who share
a common history;
Acknowledge a common authority;
face a common danger, and
expect a common future;
They agree on what work needs to
be done and who the enemy is.

Through **GOLD PRIDE** we are attempting to establish a tradition of excellence as indicated by Krzyzewski and establish relationships with you, have you develop an authentic sense of who you are as a person, build interpersonal relationships with your teammates and coaches, and find your purpose in your relationship with Christ.

In coming together as a group of student athletes it is the hope that every student athlete will begin an incredible journey that will lead them to a quality collegiate experience but more important to a lifetime of significance.

Coming together is a beginning
Understanding the vision brings perspective

Stat Sheet

Fundamentals: Basic Skills

1. "The culture we create permeates everything we touch."
   - What is the meaning of this phrase for you?

2. Adopt, adapt, adept
   - Discuss how can use this tool to develop the **GOLD PRIDE** culture?

Strength and Conditioning Training: Improving Your Shape

1. List and discuss two things in each of the categories of pursuing excellence that you want to concentrate on at this time in your collegiate experience?
   - Academic
   - Athletic
   - Building the character qualities of Christ

Game Day: Performing with Excellence

1. In what area of your life can you display more empathy?
2. Where in the past three weeks have you demonstrated excellence?
3. To emulate Christ means to serve others, the value of being selfless. Give two examples where you have demonstrated this recently?

Endnotes

[1]   Jay Bilas. *Toughness Developing True Strength On and Off the Court*. New American Library: 2013, 185.
[2]   Mike Krzyzewski. *Leading With the Heart*. Warner Books: 2001, 44.

Working Together Is Progress

Collaborative team members, completing one another is more important than competing with one another.
—James Maxwell

Several years ago, an outstanding NBA basketball player by the name of Allen Iverson did an interview that has been replayed many, many times. Iverson was a player that could be referred to as a "gamer"; this term means that when the lights go on, game day, he turns it on. However, he is not a big proponent of practice. In fact, in the interview, he made several statements about the coach's concern that he did not practice well. The dialogue went something like this, "Practice, he is talking about practice. What is practice? Practice? He is talking about practice." Allen Iverson, at least in this situation, did not understand the value of working together through practice to develop individual skills in order to become a team.

A tea bag by itself does not have much value. Put the tea bag in water and the elements in the tea bag interact with the water to begin to develop flavor and color. The result is collaboration of substances that combine to make tea. Just as the tea bag does not have much value unless it interacts with the water, you will not benefit from *The Ripple Effect* unless you invest yourself in the concepts presented and apply them to your life.

In adopting a thought, idea, or concept, you adopt it at face value. You do not resist the change in thinking but merely are open to the potential of the thought. To change requires new thinking. You need to learn the concept of replacement, to refocus. This is the ability to create better thoughts. Instead of resisting change or rebelling against the change replace it. You can change the way you feel by changing the way you think. You cannot control your feelings, but you can control what you think, which in turn will change the way you act. By keeping your motives aligned with doing the best for those around you, you will keep yourself focused on being a positive influence.

Look beyond yourself, focusing on your teammates and where you should be going together. Your focus should be on building into the members of your team, building relationships. Truett Cathy, the entrepreneur of Chick-fil-A said, "The number one reason leaders (people, student athlete, etc.) are unsuccessful is their inability to lead themselves. Leadership that regenerates is what allows people to be successful consistently. People that are willing to place the focus somewhere other than on themselves are truly unique."

Character needs to be developed from the inside out. You need to be proactive. You cannot have personal change unless you have a change of character. Character change requires courage; courage is seen in action, responsibility and accountability. John Wooden said, "You need to have courage to be true to yourself to reach your true potential." The price you are willing to pay is relative to the value you attribute to something. Remember nothing good is ever accomplished without sacrifice. If you learn to discipline yourself then others will not have to.

Working together is about a progression of taking you from dependence to independence to interdependence. A dependent person needs the validation of others in everything that they do. You need others to get what you want. In other words, you are directed, nurtured, and sustained by others. The paradigm for you is, you take care of me, you come through for me and if you do not come through for me I blame you for the results.

As an independent person, you have the ability to make your own choices or decision. You are free from the control of others. You become inner-directed and self-reliant. It is an attitude of "I," I can do it, I am responsible, I am self-reliant, I can choose. True independence of character empowers you to act rather than be acted upon. It frees you from your dependence on circumstances and other people and is a worthy goal. But it is not the ultimate goal in effective living. Unfortunately, in our society today far too many student athletes remain in this independent stage. When this occurs, many times a sense of entitlement develops. Entitlement creates an inward self-focused, self-centered person. The sheer nature of the message is the importance, rights, and benefits they deserve. They become the focus and the means to the end. God is reduced to someone who helps them get what they believe they are entitled to. This entitlement leads them to believe God owes them something; that He is in some way entitled to give them what they want. They have a right to abundance, comfort, and no problems. The tag line for this person is, "I do not have a problem with entitlement; the problem is I am not getting everything I want."

Within the athletic culture, entitlement can be expressed with these sayings, "I deserve this because I am an athlete, I have a right to this platform," or "I am entitled to this position." The outcome of this approach is the development of an attitude called "the disease of me." This entitlement reflects itself by the athlete believing they should have special treatment just because they are an athlete or that normal rules do not apply to them because they have been blessed with exceptional athletic gifts. "The disease me" is the single biggest threat to any team. It fosters bad pride or false pride in the team. The team's words or actions reflect a look at me mentality. Arrogance is prevalent since the focus of each person is on themselves there is a feeling of each being under-appreciated; cliques are formed on teams where entitlement exists, there is an environment of manipulation and relationships are non-trusting.

Interdependency is the ability to establish quality relationships with others. It is a paradigm of we, we can do it, we can cooperate, and we can combine our talents and abilities and create something greater together. As an interdependent person you have the opportunity to share yourself deeply, meaningfully, with others, and have access to the vast resources and potential of your teammates. Interdependence is a choice only independent people can make. Dependent people cannot choose to become interdependent. They do not have the character to do it; they do not own enough of themselves. When you move from independence to interdependence, you have the ability to put the needs of others ahead of your own. You have realized and learned that together we are better. You have a better understanding of yourself and how others influenced by you produce insight and empathy for you, your teammates and your other relationships as well as your relationship with Christ.

This is a sign of maturity; an interdependent person is one that models maturity. Maturity is having an accurate view of yourself; it is knowing who you are and who you are not; it is knowing what your strengths and weakness are; what the purpose of your life is and what your purpose of life is not; you know and understand your past and you do not run from it; you are a product of your past but not a prisoner of it; your past is your past but it is not your destiny; you cannot use problems in your past to affect your identity; you can make choices to move past your past. If you do not understand who you are you will not have confidence and if you do not have confidence you will not be able to do what God made you to be in developing relationships with Him or other people.

In this world of give and take, however, there are not enough people who are willing to give what it takes. Working together requires change, challenges, and choices. Change is inevitable but growth is optional. You must learn to deal with changes in your life and your lifestyle. Challenges may be more dramatic than the changes. No matter what season of life you are in you will always have challenges. To accept your challenges and to overcome them you always need to know what resources are available to you, your ability to use resources is critical. Choices, however, are where the rubber meets the road. You will always face change and challenges but the choices you make will determine your path.

We tend to make choices or decisions in four ways:

1. Circumstances: an example of this would be when you are driving and you need to determine if you should stop as the light turns yellow or continue to go through the light. The circumstances dictate what choice you will make.
2. Convenience: this is simply making a choice on what is the simplest or easiest to do.
3. Criticism: this choice is made on what others might think.
4. Convictions: this is the best way to make a choice because it is made on deeply held beliefs or values that guide your life.

One day, you will be asked to give an account of the choices you made in your life. "Each of us will have to give a personal account to God" (Romans 14:12). To whom do you want to be accountable?

You need to work to develop convictions through **GOLD PRIDE**.

There are three ways to form an agreement:

1. Contract: A formal agreement that says if you do this, I will do that.
2. Covenant: An agreement with yourself that you will do something.
3. Conviction: A deeply held belief that guides your life. A covenant that has developed into a habit that becomes part of your lifestyle.
4. Through aggressive convictions:

- Your values are clear; your decisions are easy.
- Your impact for God increases.
- You develop spiritual consistency (integrity which means whole).
- You eliminate distractions.
- You eliminate detractors.
- You eliminate doubt.
- Through your spiritual development you will learn understand how to strike and maintain a sense of balance in a world full of our ever shifting desire.
- You will no longer feel a need to justify your behavior, and you will develop a new respect for who you are as a person, student athlete and teammate.

You determine your own success by the standards you set and the choices you make. **GOLD PRIDE** will help you determine the standards that can impact your behavior. It seems in our culture today you as an individual have more freedom and more information available to you. However, many of you do not know what to do with this information or freedom. Each student athlete needs to utilize their freedom provided as a follower of Christ to adhere to the **GOLD PRIDE** standards. You do not want to be a carbon copy of collegiate culture. "Don't use this freedom as an excuse to do whatever you want to do . . . Rather, use your freedom to serve one another in love" (Galatians 5:13). There are three ways to use your freedom to make choices: (1) waste your opportunity to pursue excellence and choose not to make

the sacrifices necessary to reach significance; (2) resist your opportunity to pursue excellence and choose not to take ownership of the **GOLD PRIDE** standards to reach significance; (3) invest in your opportunity to pursue excellence and choose to live by the **GOLD PRIDE** standards to reach significance. Realize God shaped you to be you. "Do not let the world around you squeeze you into its own mold, but let God remold your mind from within, so that you may prove in practice that God's plan for you is good, meets all His demands and moves toward the goal of maturity" (Romans 12:2).

Few experiences can be as powerful as a group of student athletes being a part of a selfless group, working toward a common goal. To achieve this goal involves certain *choices* that are in the *control* of team members. *You! Realize* the power of "WE" is greater than the power of "ME." *Realize* that more people equals more resources, ideas, energy, and more potential. *Realize* that all roles are equal and sharing in the victories and defeats.

Realize you can be a part of something *bigger* than yourself. "Everybody needs friendship, encouragement, and help. What people can accomplish by themselves is almost nothing compared to their potential when working with others. And doing things with other people tends to bring contentment."[1]

Ecclesiastes 4:9–12

[9]Two are better than one, because they
have a good return for their labor:
[10]If either of them falls down,
one can help the other up.

But pity anyone who falls
and has no one to help;
[11]Also, if two lie down together,
they will keep warm.
But how can one keep warm alone?
[12]Though one may be overpowered,
two can defend themselves.
A cord of three strands is
not quickly broken.

People who try to do everything themselves alone often get themselves into trouble. One of the wildest stories I have ever seen on this subject came from the insurance claim form of a bricklayer who got hurt at a building site. He was trying to get a load of bricks down from the top floor of a building without asking for help from anyone else. He wrote:

It would have taken too long to carry all the bricks down by hand, so I decided to put them in a barrel and lower them by a pulley which I had fastened to the top of the building. After tying the rope securely at ground level, I then went up to the top of the building; I fastened the rope around the barrel, loaded it with bricks, and swung it over the sidewalk for the descent. Then I went down to the sidewalk and untied the rope, holding it securely to guide the barrel down slowly. But since I weigh only 140 pounds, the 500 pound load jerked me from the ground so fast that I did not have time to think of letting go of the rope. As I passed between the second and third floors I met the barrel coming down. This accounts for the bruises and the lacerations on my upper body.

I held tightly to the rope until I reached the top where my hand became jammed in the pulley. This accounts for my broken thumb.

At the same time, however, the barrel hit the sidewalk with a bang and the bottom fell out. With the weight of the bricks gone, the barrel weighed only about 40 pounds. Thus, my 140 pound body began a swift descent, and I met the empty barrel coming up. This accounts for my broken ankle.

Slowed only slightly, I continued the descent and landed on the pile of bricks. This accounts for my sprained back and broken collar bone.

At this point I lost my presence of mind completely, and I let go of the rope and the empty barrel came crashing down on me. This accounts for my head injuries.

And as for the last question on you insurance form, "What would I do if this situation rose again?" Please be advised I am finished trying to do the job all by myself."[2]

"Great challenges require great teamwork, and the quality most needed among teammates amid the pressure of a difficult challenge is collaboration. Notice I did not say 'cooperation' because collaboration is more than that. Cooperation is working together agreeably. Collaboration is working together aggressively.

Collaborative teammates do more than just work with one another. Each person brings something to the table that adds value to the relationship and synergy to the team. The sum of truly collaborative teamwork is always greater than its parts."[3] This is an example of the trigger, "being part of something bigger than yourself."

COMING together is a beginning. Understanding the vision brings perspective

WORKING together is progress Moving from dependence to independence to interdependence.

Stat Sheet

Fundamentals: Basic Skills

1. In adopting a thought, idea, or concept you adopt it at face value. You do not resist the change in thinking. To change requires new thinking. You need to learn the concept of replacement (to refocus).
2. "The number one reason leaders (people, student athlete, etc.) are unsuccessful is their inability to lead themselves.
3. Few experiences can be as powerful as a group of student athletes being a part of a selfless group, working toward a common goal.
4. Four ways to make choices or decision
   - Circumstances
   - Convenience
   - Criticism
   - Convictions

5. Three ways to form an agreement
   - Contract
   - Covenant
   - Conviction

6. Working together is about a progression of taking you from being dependent to independent to interdependent.
   - What is interdependence to you?

7. Read this statement below and discuss how you can incorporate this into you team?

"Great challenges require great teamwork, and the quality most needed among teammates amid the pressure of a difficult challenge is collaboration. Notice I did not say 'cooperation' because collaboration is more than that. Cooperation is working together agreeably. Collaboration is working together aggressively.

Collaborative teammates do more than just work with one another. Each person brings something to the table that adds value to the relationship and synergy to the team. The sum of truly collaborative teamwork is always greater than its parts."[4] This is an example of the trigger, "being part of something bigger than yourself."

Strength and Conditioning Training: Improving Your Shape

1. As you move from dependency to independency to interdependence you will need to establish covenants. A covenant is an agreement with yourself that you will do something. List three covenants that you would like to develop during this year.

2. A conviction is a deeply held belief that guides your life. It is a covenant that has been developed into a habit that has become part of your lifestyle. Of the three covenants listed above which one could you develop into a conviction, why and how?

Game Day: Performing with Excellence

1. Challenging cultural wrongs is one of the greatest challenges you will face as a collegiate student athlete. We let cultural expectations become our standard, we allow ourselves to be squeezed into a mold, with little room for Christ like character and competence. We live in a culture that wants to tell us how to act, how to think, how to look, and how to talk. It wants to tell us what to wear, what to buy, and where to buy it. It wants to tell us what to dream, what to value and what to live for.

- What convictions do you currently possess in your character that will keep you from conforming to cultural standards?
- Do you currently have enough convictions to be a person of significance and why?

Endnotes

1   James Maxwell. *Becoming a Person of Influence.* Nashville: Thomas Nelson, 1997, 108.
2   James Maxwell. *Becoming a Person of Influence.* Nashville: Thomas Nelson, 1997, 108–109.
3   James Maxwell. *The 17 Essential Qualities of A Team Player.* Nashville: Thomas Nelson, 1997,13–14.
4   James Maxwell. *The 17 Essential Qualities of A Team Player.* Nashville: Thomas Nelson, 1997,13–14.

Thinking Together Is Success

Character is a victory, not a gift.
—Ivor Griffith

"I beg you, brothers and sisters . . . to be completely joined together by having the same kind of thinking and the same purpose" (1 Corinthians 1:10).

Adapting means that you make modification in the thought you accepted at face value. You apply your own values, principles and standards (rules of the road) to modify the original thought. A standard is defined as a norm or requirement that establishes criteria for methods, processes, or practices. It is a reference point against which other things can be evaluated. Standards are morals, ethics, and/or habits established by authority, custom, or an individual as acceptable practices of principles. Quality standards are recognized as a model of excellence. Standards become the boundaries necessary for a student athlete. Rules are meant to be broken. With standards, you rise to set the bar high. It is important that through *The Ripple Effect* you fully understand the **GOLD PRIDE** standards (the rules of the road) and the focus necessary to uphold these standards.

Standards (academic, athletic, and in character building) are necessary to help you as a student athlete improve in your ability to make quality choices to make your collegiate experience more significant. Thinking together allows a better focus to define what is most important to you. Until you achieve this focus you will live your life in a haze of others directed urgencies. If you are always striving to achieve success with your own standards or expectations that have been defined by someone else or another athletic program or what society says is the way to do it, there will be frustration and there will be violations of team standards.

As a student athlete, we need to be all of identical mind as we begin to think together for the success of your sport, your teammates, and your eternity. You need to battle together for the development of your character and your spiritual formation. You cannot have personal change unless you have a change of character; you can be more than what you have become.

When pressure (temptation) comes you allow what is inside to come out (character). Will this be a bad reflection of you or will your character allow you to respond appropriately? You need others that have the same values to hold you accountable. "I can will it, but cannot do it. I decide to do good, but I do not really do it; I decide not to do bad, but then I do it anyway. My decisions, such as they are, do not result in actions. Something has gone wrong deep within me and gets the better of me every time" (Romans 7:17–18). Rather than react you need to be able to respond because you apply the same set of personal standards to every situation regardless of how large or small, private or public. Michael Josephson said, "One of the ultimate tests of personal character is the willingness and ability to do the right thing despite the cost and risks— to do it without any expectation of approval or advantage, but simply because it is the right thing to do."

"The temptations in your life are not different from what others experience. God is faithful. He will not allow the temptation to be more than you can stand. When you are tempted, He will show you a way out so that you can endure" (1 Corinthians 10:13). Being together in Christ is more than belief, it is a belong system. "First they gave themselves to the Lord; and then, by God's will they gave themselves to us (each other) as well" (2 Corinthians 8:5). You cannot fulfill God's purpose for yourself until you until to learn to love God and others; people connecting, thinking together to love God and each other.

Mark Driscoll said, "Most of our life is spent creating and defending an identity that will ultimately fail. Beauty will fade, wealth will disappear, relationships will crumble, and health will decline. If your identity is anything other than 'God made me' and 'Jesus saved me,' you are in for disappointment, despair, and destruction. Your identity shapes your entire life, so choose carefully."

We use the educational methodology to introduce and teach the **GOLD PRIDE** standards. Our approach is intentional as student athletes come together and begin to work together. We **define** the standards because we believe you will follow what you are asked to focus on. We **model** the standards by applying the foundational premises of **GOLD PRIDE**, providing an example that in everything we do our actions follow our principles or values. We **shape** the standards because if you are not being directed you will drift in your commitments. Great leaders instill a sense of meaning and belonging in their followers by putting a personal imprint of who they are and what they stand for on their people. That imprint becomes the common ground where people collectively meet and identify with the mission. Finally, we **reinforce** the standards because what is rewarded leads to positive habits and traditions.

"Most people tend to associate commitment (thinking together) with their emotions. If they feel the right way, then they can follow through on their commitments. But true commitment does not work that way. It is not emotion; it is a character quality that enables us to reach our goals. Human emotions go up and down all the time, but commitment has to be rock solid."[1] You must have members of your team on the same page with the same thought process for commitment to achieve significance.

Thinking together is not dependent on your talent or abilities. It comes as a result of a choice based on values. Many times we believe something to be true without the proper thought process. Sometimes in your collegiate experience you allow conditions to affect your thinking that determine your choices; this is why your choices need to be thoughtful and based on values.

Thinking together requires you to find the truth in your thinking. Thinking great thoughts is a deliberate, intentional process of informing your mind with truth. Thoughts that are derived from value system that reflects the truth are more likely lived out.

Philippians 4:8–9 illustrates what "thinking together" is about: "Summing it all up, friends, I'd say you'll do best by filling your minds and meditating on things true, noble, reputable, authentic, compelling, gracious—the best, not the worst; the beautiful, not the ugly; things to praise, not things to curse. Put into practice what you learned from me, what you heard and saw and realized. Do that, and God, who makes everything work together, will work you into His most excellent harmonies."

Coming together is a beginning
Understanding the vision brings perspective

Working together is progress
Moving from dependence to independence to interdependence

Thinking together is success
Establishes commitment and collective purpose

Stat Sheet

Fundamentals: Basic Skills

1. Adapting means that you make modification in the thought you accepted at face value. You apply your own values, principles, and standards to modify the original thought.

2. A standard is defined as a norm or requirement that establishes criteria for methods, processes or practices. It is a reference point against which other things can be evaluated. Standards are morals, ethics, habits established by authority, custom, or an individual as acceptable practices of principles. Quality standards are recognized as a model of excellence.

3. Standards (academics, athletics, and character building) are necessary to help our student athletes improve their ability to make quality choices using the **GOLD PRIDE** standards and values to help make their collegiate experience more significant.

4. Thinking together allows a better focus to define what is most important to you; until you achieve this focus you will live your life in a haze of others directed urgencies.

5. Thinking together is not dependent on your talent or abilities. It comes as a result of a choice based on values.

6. Define yourself in terms of the paragraph listed below:

When pressure (temptation) comes you allow what is inside to come out (character). Will this be a bad reflection of you or will your character allow you to respond appropriately? You need others that have the same values to hold you accountable. "I can will it, but cannot do it. I decide to do good, but I do not really do it; I decide not to do bad, but then I do it anyway. My decisions, such as they are, do not result in actions. Something has gone wrong deep within me and gets the better of me every time." (Romans 7:17–18). Rather than react you need to be able to respond because you apply the same set of personal standards to every situation regardless of how large or small, private or public. Michael Josephson said, "One of the ultimate tests of personal character is the willingness and ability to do the right thing despite the cost and risks—

to do it without any expectation of approval or advantage, but simply because it is the right thing to do."

Strength and Conditioning Training: Improving Your Shape

1. Philippians 4:8 says, "Finally, brothers, whatever is true, whatever is honorable, whatever is right, whatever is pure, whatever is lovely, whatever is admirable, if there is any excellent or anything worthy of praise, think about these things."
   - In this passage think about the concepts presented and take into account what is said about character and realize the implication that are here for your life.

Paul is telling believers that whatever is characterized by these godly qualities is worthy of a lot of active meditation. In other words, he tells them to think great thoughts.

- TRUE
  - o Think about things that are objectively true
  - o Things that conform to reality
  - o Before you put something in your mind—ask yourself:
  Is it true?
- HONORABLE
  - o This word means worthy of respect.
  - o It refers to those things that reflect the serious purpose of a believer's life
  - o Before that movie, commercial or conversation goes into your mind ask yourself: Does this honor God and reflect His purpose for me?
- RIGHT
  - o This word implies justice and righteousness
  - o In the New Testament, it is used to refer to the character and actions of the Father and Jesus.
  - o It is a picture of duty
  - o Before you spend time thinking about something, ask yourself: Is this right or wrong?
- PURE
  - o It comes from the same root word of holy and means to be pure from defilement of immorality.
  - o It carries the idea of internal integrity
  - o Ask yourself: am I thinking on things that are pure and holy?
- LOVELY
  - o It means attractive, winsome, or beautiful.
  - o It pictures things that call forth a response of love and warmth from within us.
  - o Ask yourself: Is my mind filled with beauty?

- ADMIRABLE
  - o The general sense of the word is "admirable" but its literal meaning is "fair speaking"
  - o In other words are these thoughts fit for God's hearing?
- ANYTHING OF EXCELLENCE AND WORTHY OF PRAISE
  - o These last two thoughts are a summary category for anything that has moral excellence, motivates us to godly behavior, or encourages other to walk with God.
- What Paul is saying is get your thoughts right and the emotions, behaviors, and consequences of peace will follow.
- Are you thinking great thoughts about yourself, your teammates, and your collegiate experience as a means of moving toward significance? Describe how what Paul has described above can help you become a better you?

Game Day: Performing with Excellence

1. A group of individuals that think together develop a shared joy of participation together. There is a kind of feeling that develops between all the individuals (team members) that no one on the outside can understand. This phenomenon is called an "inner circle."
- Shared joy involves
  - o A desire to become as good as possible for yourself and the team
  - o It attempts to take ordinary things and make something special out of them
  - o Trusting relationships
  - o Teammates are accountable to each other
  - o Teammates communicate with the truth being the basis for all they do
- Through the inner circle the following traits are present
  - o Unselfishness (teammates can be counted on)
  - o Ownership of their behavior (accountability)
  - o Determination to prepare (work habits)
  - o Demonstration of humility (I do not need to bring attention to myself)
  - o Felt in parts of the game where there is more effort and determination than skill
  - o An inner circle is not developed on poorly disciplined teams
  - o Never find a quality inner circle where the leaders of that team put winning above character

- Results of Good Pride
  - o Team Toughness
  - o Common bonds formed because of high trust level
  - o A commitment for what the team stands for
  - o Are you a part of a team that has the characteristics of an inner circle? If so why? If not why not? If not what can you do to help improve the situation?

Endnotes

1. James Maxwell. *The 17 Essential Qualities of A Team Player*. Nashville: Thomas Nelson, 1997, 22.

Believing Together Is Significance

THIS IS WHAT WE BELIEVE; THEREFORE, THIS IS WHAT YOU WILL SEE

In our society today there is a crisis of lack of integrity, lack of respect, lack of responsibility, and lack of role models (influencers). Pat Williams in his book, *American Scandal*, describes it this way:

We have taller buildings but shorter tempers. We spend more but have less. We buy more but enjoy less. We have bigger houses and smaller families, more conveniences but less time. We have more degrees but less sense, more knowledge but less judgment, more experts but more problems, more medicine but less wellness.

We have multiplied our possessions but reduced our values. We talk too much, love seldom, and hate too often. We have learned how to make a living but not a life. We have added years to life, not life to years. We have been all the way to the moon and back but have trouble crossing the street to meet a new neighbor. We have conquered outer space but not inner peace. We have cleaned up the air but polluted the soul. We have split the atom but not our prejudice. We have higher incomes but lower morals.

These are times of tall men and short character; steep profits and shallow relationships. These are times of world peace but domestic warfare. These are days of two incomes but more divorce, fancier houses but broken homes.

Does this sound like the type of world you want to live in?"[1]

The message in this passage occurs because of the selfishness that exists in society. We want what we want for ourselves. A. W. Tozer once said, "The reason why many are still troubled, still seeking, still making little forward progress is because they have not yet come to the end of themselves."[2] This is what makes believing together the most difficult "together" to achieve. To be a part of a group that has become selfless and emulates Christ in their pursuit of excellence is not a common occurrence. *Becoming selfless is a process that involves surrendering. Surrender is defined, to yield (something) to the power of another.*

To become adept at something you take the original thought and make it part of your approach that fits you and your needs. Believing together is a process that occurs if each person collectively invests in their character and spiritual formation, the inevitable result is growth over time. Although we are all gifted with different skills, some more than others, the ability to become better than you are is a product of *The Ripple Effect*. The investment and learning process has many facets. To move from success to significance in your character development and spiritual formation is an ongoing process that is a result of self-discipline and perseverance. The goal each day is to get a little better, to build on the previous day's progress.

The greatest missing ingredient in athletics today is credibility. The ability to model or match your behavior on the sidelines as well on the sidewalks; to be an authentic student athlete you need to be consistent. You cannot represent what is right in competition and then exhibit a different lifestyle that demonstrates a lack of character off the field or court of play. At the same time, you cannot represent what is right in your life away from the diamond or track and exhibit a lack of character in the competitive arena.

What happens to you in life is not as important as the choices you make about what happens to you. Your choices determine who you are, what you believe, and your character. Decisions determine your destiny. You are free to make any choice you want but you are not free from the consequences of that choice; once you make the choice, you are no longer free but must be accountable for that choice.

The lens on how you perceive your life is critical for growth. A person who says they can or says they cannot are both right. One has faith and one does not. One lives their life by faith and the other with fear. What you believe to be true shapes who you are. "If I asked how you picture life, what image would come to your mind? That image is your life metaphor. It is the view of life you hold, consciously or unconsciously, in your mind. It is your description of how life works and what you expect from it."[3] It is what you believe to be true about yourself, your support system, your relationships, your values, your expectations, everything about you. It is what you believe.

However, knowledge + belief – Action = Zero (no significance). To have the knowledge of what should be done (coming and working together) plus a belief that this is the correct way to pursue excellence (thinking together) without action that meets the appropriate standards (this is what we believe, therefore this is what you will see) equals zero (lack of maturity, character, spiritual formation, and the results are low expectations for your collegiate experience).

Believing together calls for you to live by a higher standard; being faithful to God and the **GOLD PRIDE** standard is a choice; that choice is being obedient. Choices are the hinges of destiny. You need to make sure your decision to be obedient enhances your destiny.

These characteristics are present in a life that chooses to be obedient and pursue a life with God's higher standards:

1. Godly values are present in your life
2. A greater care for the interest of others
3. You live with greater integrity
4. You develop your potential with your gifts and talents
5. Life is not easier but simpler because your life has direction

Philippians 2:1–16 illustrates what believing together is all about:

"If you've gotten anything at all out of following Christ, if His love has made any difference in your life, if being in a community of the Spirit means anything to you, if you have a heart, if you care—then do me a favor: Agree with each other, love each other, be deep-spirited friends. Don't push your way to the front; don't sweet talk your way to the top. Put yourself aside, and help others get ahead. Don't be obsessed with getting your own advantage. Forget yourselves long enough to lend a helping hand. Think of yourselves the way Christ Jesus thought of Himself. He had equal status with God but didn't think so much of Himself that He had to cling to the advantages of that status no matter what. Not at all. When the time came, He set aside the privileges of deity and took on the status of a slave, became human! Having become human, He stayed human. It was an incredibly humbling process. He didn't claim special privileges. Instead, He lived a selfless, obedient life and then died a selfless, obedient death—and the worst kind of death at that: a crucifixion. Because of that obedience, God lifted Him high and honored Him far beyond anyone or anything, ever, so that all created beings in heaven and on earth—even those long ago dead and buried—will bow in worship before this Jesus Christ, and call out in praise that He is the Master of all, to the glorious honor of God the Father. What I'm getting at, friends, is that you should simply keep on doing what you've done from the beginning. When I was living among you, you lived in responsive obedience. Now that I'm separated from you, keep it up. Better yet, redouble your efforts. Be energetic in your life of salvation, reverent and sensitive before God. That energy is God's energy, energy deep within you, God Himself willing and working at what will give Him the most pleasure. Do everything readily and cheerfully—no bickering, no second-guessing allowed! Go out into the world uncorrupted, a breath of fresh air in this squalid and polluted society. Provide people with a glimpse of good living and of the living God. Carry the light-giving Message into the night."

Kelly Schmidt, a Vanguard University alum, who was the NAIA Women's Basketball Player of the Year in 2004–2005, a four-time NAIA All American and the Dr. Leroy Walker Award winner in 2006–2007 (the NAIA student athlete of character) made this comment about the development of her character and spiritual formation:

It is difficult to explain what my collegiate experience as a student athlete has meant to me. I can say I am a completely different person than I was when I came to college. One of the most important things I learned is to have a life that didn't just revolve around basketball but to become a well-rounded person. To achieve this balance, I took many things that I had learned from basketball and incorporated them into other parts of my life. At the same time, I brought things from other parts of my life into basketball, and that is why I embraced the concept of changing the culture of sport. To truly be a person of character is a choice. A person cannot select when to exhibit character and when not to, character needs to be part of every area of your life all the time, including sports. The five core character values provide a great model of what an athlete should look like, but also what a person should look like in life.

The culture we create permeates everything we touch.
—Tony Dungy

COMING together is a beginning
Understanding the vision brings perspective

WORKING together is progress
Moving from dependence to independence to interdependence

THINKING together is success
Establishes commitment and collective purpose

BELIEVING together is significance
Defining your legacy

From the sideline, to the sidewalk, to significance

Stat Sheet

Fundamentals: Basic Skills

1. To become adept at something you take the original thought and make it part of your approach that fits you and your needs.
2. A. W. Tozer once said, "The reason why many are still troubled, still seeking, still making little forward progress is because they have not yet come to the end of themselves."
3. Believing together is a process that occurs if each person collectively invests in their character and spiritual formation, the inevitable result is growth over time
4. The greatest missing ingredient in athletics today is credibility. The ability to model or match your behavior on the sidelines as well in the sidewalks; to be an authentic student athlete you need to be consistent.
5. The lens on how you perceive your life is critical for growth.
6. Knowledge + Belief – Action = Zero (no significance).
7. Believing together calls for you to live by a higher standard; being faithful to God and the **GOLD PRIDE** standard is a choice; that choice is being obedient.

How can you use the basic skill list here of believing together to define your legacy?

Strength and Conditioning Training: Improving Your Shape

1. To be a part of a group that believes in each other you need to know your SHAPE
   - **Strengths**
     o Need to know your strengths in all the components of your potential (see potential section)
     o **List those strengths and discuss why they have become strength for you.**
   - **Heart**
     o Your heart reflects your passion
     o From the heart flow moral courage, conviction, and consciences as well as compassion and character

- o Need to answer these things about yourself
- o Can you be trusted?
- o Are you committed to excellence?
- o Do you care about your teammates?

- **Attitude**
  - o Do you have a teachable spirit and are you loyal?
  - o Will you take ownership of **GOLD PRIDE**

- **Personality**
  - o Does your personality fit with your teammates?

- **Experiences**
  - o Can you blend your experiences with your teammates to making your collegiate experience successful and move toward living significantly?

Game Day: Performing with Excellence

1. Believing together calls for you to live by a higher standard; be making your collegiate experience successful and being faithful to God and the **GOLD PRIDE** standard is a choice; that choice is being obedient. Choices are the hinges of destiny. You need to make sure your decision to be obedient enhances your destiny.

2. These characteristics are present in a life that chooses to be obedient and pursue a life with God's higher standards:
   - Godly values are present in your life
   - A greater care for the interest of others
   - You live with greater integrity
   - You develop your potential with your gifts and talents
   - Life is not easier but simpler because your life has direction

3. **Using these criteria describe in detail how can you become a more complete competitor, a better GOLD PRIDE teammate?**

Endnotes

1 Pat Williams. *American Scandal.* Destiny Image, 2003, 15.
2 Rick Warren. *What on Earth Am I Here For?* Zondervan: 2013, 81.
3 Rick Warren. *What on Earth Am I Here For?* Zondervan: 2013, 44–45.

Section V

Better Together

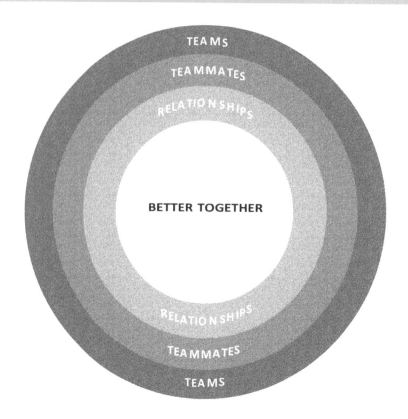

Ownership of Gold Pride

Relationships develop by coming together, working together, thinking together and believing together. You need to realize that there is purpose for everyone you meet. Some will test you, some will use you, and some will teach you.

But most importantly, some will bring out the best in you. Never neglect the people who are most important to you simply because you think they will always be there. In relationships, distance is not measured in miles but in knowing and understanding each other. Appreciate and be affectionate with those who truly matter to you; not because it is convenient, but because they are worth the extra effort. Section V is learning how to put the principles discussed to this point into action and discover that we are better together.

Relationships Teammates-Teams

There are two keys that determine who we are: who we conceive ourselves to be and who we associate with.
—Anonymous

"Relationships help us to define who we are and what we can become. Most of us can trace our successes to pivotal relationships."[1]

Much of being a quality teammate and developing quality relationships are a result of having a proper attitude. Improper attitudes in your relationships will reduce your ability to develop a connection with others and thus hinder your ability to be able to reach your true potential.

This is what is needed to be part of a team driven by Christ's values

1. **T**rust: Being of like mind; sharing responsibility; understanding that all roles are equal.
2. **E**mpathy: Seeking first to understand then to be understood; be a good communicator.
3. **A**ccept: Being of one spirit.
4. **M**ission: Having the same purpose, to love God with all your heart and love others as Yourself.

Frederic F. Flach once wrote, "Most people look back over the years and identify a time and place at which their lives changed significantly. Whether by accident or design, these are moments when, because of a readiness within us, and collaboration with events occurring around us, we are focused to seriously reappraise ourselves and the conditions under which we live and to make certain that will affect the rest of our lives."[2] "Far too many people think that conditions determine choices. More often, choices determine conditions. When you choose commitment you give yourself a chance for success."[3]

Relationships are the glue that holds the team together—the more solid the relationships, the more cohesive the team. Ripple effects in developing relationships include **respect, shared experiences, trust, reciprocity,** and **mutual enjoyment**. When it comes to developing relationships everything begins with respect. Respect is valuing the person or situation that stands before you. Respect is the value you place on something or someone; you need to place value on those you want to have a relationship with. Les Giblin said, "You cannot make the other fellow feel important in your presences if you secretly feel that he is a nobody."[4] Respecting each other is only the beginning. "Respect can lay the foundation of a good relationship, but it alone is not enough. You cannot be relational with someone you do not know. It requires shared experiences that are developed over time."[5] "You will never develop common ground with your teammates unless you share common experiences."[6] As you spend time with someone you respect you begin to develop a trust for that person and the development of trust enhances a relationship. "Scottish poet George Macdonald observed, 'To be trusted is a greater compliment than to be loved.' Without trust, you cannot sustain any kind of relationship."[7] Quality relationships need reciprocity, which is the practice of exchanging things with others for mutual benefits. Therefore, for a quality relationship there needs to be give and take on both parts. St. Francis of Assisi once said, "All getting separates you from others; all giving unites to others." Promote your teammate rather than yourself; practice taking a subordinate role; give secretly. John Bunyan once said, "You have not lived today successfully unless you have done something for someone who can never repay you." The concept of win-win is important in the development of reciprocity in the development of relationships with teammates. Finally, for any relationship to be solid the people involved need to enjoy each other. They need to enjoy being together, working together, and the benefits and accomplishments of their relationships.

The development of teams and being a quality teammate needs to be done intentionally and with purpose. Earlier in this manual, we stated the definition of a tribe: the definition is worth repeating now because it gives us a parameter to begin discussion on how you can develop the kind of relationship with teammates to be a part of a legacy team.

A tribe is a band of people who share a common history;
Acknowledged a common authority;
Faced a common danger, and expected common future;
They agreed on what work needed to be done and who the enemy is.

You will always be a part of some team. You need to learn and understand that you need others. "Few people are successful unless a lot of people want them to be."[8]

Every year a team wins a championship. The best team in the NAIA wins the championship. The best high school team wins the state championship. All these teams have one thing in common. No matter how tough it became throughout their season they did on thing—they held the rope!

What is holding the rope? Imagine that you are hanging from the edge of a cliff with a drop of twenty thousand feet. The only thing between you and a fall to your death is a rope with the person of your choice on the other end. Who do you know that is going to let that rope burn his or her hand and not let go? How many people do you know that are going to withstand the burn-

ing pain and watch the blood drip from their hands for you?

If you can name two people that is not good enough because those two people might not be around; the next time your team is together, look around and ask yourself, who could I trust to hole the rope? Who is going to let their hands bleed for me? When you can look at every member of your team and say to yourself that they all would hold the rope, you are destined to win a lot of games and compete for a championship. The team that holds the rope when the going gets tough are the winners. When you are down by four points with thirty seconds to go, do not give up. Yell at your teammates to hold the rope, let it burn, and do not let go.

Every year, there are winners and losers in all sports. Every year, the winners hold the rope. You do not have to be the best on the court or field to win the game. If you play with poise and do what you have prepared to do and most of all hold the rope—you will be successful. No matter what sports you play, in order to win you have to have a commitment to your team. If you are supposed to run three miles per week, do it. If you have to lift weights three times per week, do not miss. Once you start letting up at practice or start missing your workouts, you have killed the team because you let your teammates down and did not hold the rope.

Do not let your team down. Hold the rope.

God-given ability may be out of your control, but the ability to develop yourself as a quality teammate and to work as a team is not. One key to being a quality teammate is being willing to adapt yourself to the needs of the team not to have an expectation that the team should adapt to you. A team is many people with a single heartbeat.

The **GOLD PRIDE** plan includes developing your particular sports team, as well as your **GOLD PRIDE TEAM**, in addition to helping you become a quality teammate. We are better together.

Questions your teammates will ask about you include: Can they trust you? Are you committed to the team? Do you care about them as a teammate? The atmosphere on a team (locker room environment) needs to be one of security (a high trust level). Trust is the confidence among team members that their teammate's intentions are good, and that there is no reason to be protective or careful around the group. Teams that lack trust waste large amounts of time and energy managing their behaviors and interactions within the group. Trust is knowing that when a team member does push you, they are doing it because they care about the team. Push with respect (confront in love), and under the assumption that the other person is probably doing the right thing. But push anyway. And never hold back. Trust is the foundation of real teamwork; lack of trust stems from the unwillingness to be vulner-able within the group. Team members who are not genuinely open with one another about their mistakes and weaknesses make it impossible to build a foundation of trust. Great teams do not hold back with one another. They admit mistakes, their weaknesses and their concerns without fear of reprisal. To develop team trust you need two things: to be involved and to participate. Manipulation is when people choose their words and actions based on how they want others to react rather than based on what they really think. All great relationships, the ones that last over time, require productive conflict in order to grow. Teams that lack trust are incapable of engaging in unfiltered and passionate communication.

"You beat 50 percent of the people in America by working hard. You beat another 40 percent by being a person of honesty and integrity and standing for something. The last 10 percent is a dogfight in the free enterprise system," A. L. Williams said. In developing relationships, to become a quality teammate the characteristics of being solution oriented, persistent, and tenacious are important. You need to be part of the solution, not part of the problem and have the ability to finish to be a good teammate on a legacy team.

James Maxwell relates this acronym about problems (conflict):

Predictors: They help mold our future.
Reminders: We are not self-sufficient. We need God and others to help.
Opportunities: They pull us out of our rut and cause us to think creatively.

Blessings: They open up doors that we usually do not go through.

Lessons: Each new challenge will be our teacher.

Everywhere: No place or person is excluded.

Messages: They warn us about potential disaster.

Solvable: No problem is without solution.

Many times, relationships are strengthened in the midst of adversity. Problems are always a matter of perspective, most are solvable, and they either stop you or stretch you. When problems occur this is when relationships (teammates) respond together. They refocus their thinking and rethink their strategy and determine they will not give up. They remain tenacious and persistent together. "Some people who lack tenacity do so because they mistakenly believe that being tenacious demands from them more than they have to offer. As a result, they do not push themselves. However, being tenacious requires that you give 100 percent—not more, but certainly not less. If you give your all, you afford yourself every opportunity possible for success."[9] In other words, in relationships give all you have, not more than you have. You need to work through hard times. Thomas Edison once said, "I start where the last man left off." Quality teammates that are a part of a legacy team know that when problems come it is not time to quit, but time to begin to work both harder and smarter. Their team stands for something much more important than the problem before them. The process needs to be stay on your game and do not quit until the job is completed. Do not let the good distract your team from being great.

In the context of a team, commitment is a function of clarity and ownership (buy in). Where true commitment exists there are no halfhearted champions. Commitment has sustainability when it is based on values. Expectations need to be clearly defined or the failure to buy in or take ownership of decisions result in ambiguity. The development of a legacy team involves the development of core covenants (standards). In developing standards team members have an understanding of who they are and what the team stands for. Standards are binding agreements that are clearly defined where the action is physically visible; this is what we believe, therefore this is what you will see. Standards establish what the team will compromise and what they will not. Standards set the team apart from other teams. In establishing the standards the team needs to not only identify what they stand for; they need to write the them down, make them public, practice them, make sure that they see the standards in the teams behavior and conduct at all times (win or lose) and make all decisions through the standards. Most teams do not get to this point because it takes time, effort and most students are too cool or selfish and most coaches are too busy to be intentional about developing their team.

Without committing to a clear plan of action, even the most focused and driven people often hesitate to hold their teammates accountable to their actions and behaviors that seem counterproductive to the good of the team. Members of great teams improve their relationships by holding each other accountable, thus demonstrating that they respect each other and have high expectation for one another's performance. Once clarity and ownership are set you need to hold each other accountable for high standards of performance and behavior. The most important challenge in building a team where people hold one another accountable is overcoming the understandable hesitance of human beings to give one another critical feedback. People are not going to hold each other accountable if they have not clearly bought into the same plan.

Team members cannot put their individual desires (such as ego, status on them, or recognition) above the collective goal of the team. The key is to make the collective ego greater than the individual ones.

When everyone is focused on team results and using those results to define team success, it is difficult for ego to get out of hand. The teams that figure it out have a greater advantage because most of their competitors (other teams) are just a bunch of individuals looking out for themselves. The key is to define your goals and your results, in a way that is simple enough to grasp easily, and specific enough to be put into action. Winning is not actionable enough. As soon as the reality of life or the stress of the season is reintroduced, people revert back to the behaviors that put them in the difficult situation in the first place (old habits). When we talk about focusing on team results instead of individual recognition, we are talking about everyone adopting a set of common goals, and measurements, and then actually using them to make individual and collective decisions (choices) on a daily basis. This is the essence of **GOLD PRIDE**.

The development of a quality team that works together remains the one sustainable competitive advantage that has been largely untapped. When it comes to helping people find fulfillment in their sport, there is nothing more important than teamwork. The true measure of a team is that it accomplishes the results that it sets out to achieve.

Developing a better team always begins with you. To improve the team, improve yourself. "Instead of putting others in their place, try to put yourself in their place. That is not always easy. Only when you have a sense of peace about yourself and who you are will you be able to be other-minded and give yourself away to others."[10] The key to how you treat people is how you think about them.

Belonging is especially critical to us as individuals. Belonging helps us develop our sense of identity and self-worth. To be a part of a whole greater than one's self is critical to one's wellbeing and self-discovery. Belonging is essential to the healthy emotional and social development of student athletes. Being a part of a team or community enhances both personal and collective growth. Community literally means to gift one and another. Team is a synonym for community. Team means every individual is inextricably bound to the others and to the success of the whole community. A team is a group of individuals who gift one and another with a mutual sense of authenticity, trust, care, and support. Community or team provides the necessary nutrients every student athlete needs to grow, develop, connect, and contribute. No student athlete, no matter how talented has ever won a game alone. A team is a complex organism. They are interdependent; no teammate can function without the connection with other teammates. Team players need to learn to play a role in concert with their teammates. You do not give your all to the game; you give your all to the team. In his acceptance speech for the Football Hall of Fame, Emmitt Smith said these words to Daryl Johnston, the Dallas Cowboy fullback who cleared the path for many of his runs, "You mean the world to me." The tearful Smith told Johnston, asking him to stand up and be recognized by the crowd, "Not just because we shared the same backfield, but because you sacrificed so much for me. You took care of me as though you were taking care of your little brother. Without you I know today would not have been possible. I love you from the bottom of my heart." The overridden concept of team is this WE ARE BETTER TOGETHER!

Being on a Team vs. Being a Teammate

1. Being on the team benefits your personal goals and ambitions. Being a teammate benefits the goals and ambitions of your team and your teammates.

2. Being on a team can make you a bystander. Teammates intervene in the lives and actions of their teammates.

3. Being on a team involves personal effort. Being a teammate involves the efforts of every player.

4. Being on the team means doing what is asked of you. Being a teammate is doing whatever is needed for the team to succeed.

5. Being on the team can involve blaming others and making excuses. Being a teammate involves accepting responsibility, accountability, and ownership of the team's problems.

6. Being on the team makes you "me-opic," asking what is in it for me? Being a teammate makes you "we-opic," asking what is in it for us.

7. Sometimes players on a team are drawn together by common interests; teammates are drawn together by common mission.

8. Sometimes players on a team like one another; teammates respect one another.

9. Sometimes players on a team bond together because of a shared background or compatible personalities; teammates bond together because they recognize every player is needed to accomplish the goal of the team.

10. Sometimes players on a team are energized by emotions; teammates energized one another out of commitment.[11]

There are two keys that determine who we are: who we conceive ourselves to be and who we associate with.
—Anonymous

Building quality teams and developing relationships with teammates is essential to understanding yourself. Developing relationships with your teammates that lead to establishing an inner circle with your team is what participating in athletics is about. The Bible provides wisdom about how to achieve this and why it is important. In the Bible, teamwork is not the goal; it is instead described as the visible illustration of people who are united with the same Christ.

1 Peter 4:8–10
"Above all, keep loving one another earnestly, since love covers a multitude of sins. Show hospitality to one another without grumbling. As each has received a gift, use it to serve one another, as good stewards of God's varied grace."

This verse focuses on the need for teammates to use their talents to serve others and to adapt their skills to fit the gaps that the team needs filled. Being kind and serving gladly, instead of complaining, are tremendously important skills for teammates.

Hebrews 10:24–25
"And let us consider how we may spur one another on toward love and good deeds, not giving up meeting together, as some are in the habit of doing, but encouraging one another—and all the more as you see the Day approaching."

Everyone on your team needs encouragement and wants to feel a part of something greater than themselves. Meeting together is important because, by investing time together you build the relationships and trust which create a more positive, caring and cohesive culture.

1 Corinthians 12:17–20
"If the whole body were an eye, where would the sense of hearing be? If the whole body were an ear, where would the sense of smell be? But in fact God has placed the parts in the body, every one of them, just as He wanted them to be. If they were all one part, where would the body be? As it is, there are many parts, but one body."

The best teams do not have people with similar skills—they combine the diverse talents and backgrounds from a pool of diverse individuals and appreciate the gifts that each one brings to contribute. Great teams have people that know their role and appreciate others as well.

Proverbs 27:17
"As iron sharpens iron, so one person sharpens another."

The power of leadership is best summarized in one word: influence. As teammates, our expectations and attitudes and behaviors absolutely impact those around us. We all are sharpened and improved by the interactions and examples of our teammates.

Ecclesiastes 4:9–10
"Two are better than one, because they have a good return for their labor: If either of them falls down, one can help the other up. But pity anyone who falls and has no one to help them up."

Nobody climbs Mount Everest alone. To accomplish great things, we all need teammates and a supporting cast to pick us up—and we need to look for opportunities to pick others up as well when they stumble.

Ordinary people working together as teammates intentionally to develop as a team can make an extraordinary impact on our society.

Stat Sheet

Fundamentals: Basic Skills

1. Relationships are important because they define who you are and what you can become.
2. Qualities needed to develop a good relationship are respect, shared experiences, trust, reciprocity, and mutual enjoyment.
3. All great relationships, the ones that last over time, require productive conflict in order to mature.
4. The difference between being on a team vs. being a teammate.

Which one of the ten examples of being on a team vs being a teammate has the most meaning for you? Why?

Strength and Conditioning Training: Improving Your Shape

- How are you when it comes to being a quality teammate?
- If improving your team requires you to change the way you do things, how do you react?
- Are you supportive, or would you rather do things your way?
- If someone with better talent joins your team, would you be willing to take a different role?
- To help with these questions, Bruce Brown of Proactive Coaching (www.proactivevcoaching), developed a survey to help determine your status as a good teammate. Rate yourself as to how you see yourself as a teammate, then rate how you would rate your teammates in relation to this survey, and finally, how would your teammates rate you in relation to this survey.

Are you a GOOD TEAMMATE?

RATE YOURSELF AS A GOOD TEAMMATE					HOW WOULD YOU RATE YOUR TEAMMATES					HOW WOULD YOUR TEAMMATES RATE YOU				
TEACHABLE SPIRIT					TEACHABLE SPIRIT					TEACHABLE SPIRIT				
1	2	3	4	5	1	2	3	4	5	1	2	3	4	5
WORK HABITS					WORK HABITS					WORK HABITS				
1	2	3	4	5	1	2	3	4	5	1	2	3	4	5
PRIDE and HUMILITY					PRIDE and HUMILITY					PRIDE and HUMILITY				
1	2	3	4	5	1	2	3	4	5	1	2	3	4	5
CONFIDENCE					CONFIDENCE					CONFIDENCE				
1	2	3	4	5	1	2	3	4	5	1	2	3	4	5
ACADEMIC					ACADEMIC					ACADEMIC				
1	2	3	4	5	1	2	3	4	5	1	2	3	4	5
ACCOUNTABILITY					ACCOUNTABILITY					ACCOUNTABILITY				
1	2	3	4	5	1	2	3	4	5	1	2	3	4	5
MENTAL TOUGHNESS					MENTAL TOUGHNESS					MENTAL TOUGHNESS				
1	2	3	4	5	1	2	3	4	5	1	2	3	4	5
TRUSTWORTHINESS					TRUSTWORTHINESS					TRUSTWORTHINESS				
1	2	3	4	5	1	2	3	4	5	1	2	3	4	5
SELFLESSNESS-TEAMMATE					SELFLESSNESS-TEAMMATE					SELFLESSNESS-TEAMMATE				
1	2	3	4	5	1	2	3	4	5	1	2	3	4	5
ENTHUSIASM-PASSION					ENTHUSIASM-PASSION					ENTHUSIASM-PASSION				
1	2	3	4	5	1	2	3	4	5	1	2	3	4	5
DISCIPLINE					DISCIPLINE					DISCIPLINE				
1	2	3	4	5	1	2	3	4	5	1	2	3	4	5
SPORTSMANSHIP					SPORTSMANSHIP					SPORTSMANSHIP				
1	2	3	4	5	1	2	3	4	5	1	2	3	4	5

Game Day: Performing with Excellence

Rate your team according to the following scale:

1. Academic excellence of team— team GPA, class attendance.
2. Campus leadership and involvement
3. Local Community involvement
4. Embracing the five core character values of the Champions of Character Initiative
    - RESPECT
    o Teachable spirit
        - Ability to be coached
        - Dedicated to pursuing excellence (academically, athletically, character building)
        - Team improvement during the season
        - Desire to get an education and not just a degree
        - Pursue the Vanguard University lifestyle standards
    o Work habits
        - Willing to be subjected to hard, productive work
        - Willing to make the necessary sacrifices to be prepared to work diligently every day
        - Committed to working hard to improve every area of your life
        - Conscientious in getting everything done in a timely manner

Champions of Character Team Award Criteria

o Team Development
    - Unselfishness
    - Builds positive traditions
    - Good leadership
    - Trust
    - Ownership of GOLD PRIDE: Significance
    - RESPONSIBILITY Consistency
    - Reliable in every situation
o Discipline
    - Focus on pursuing excellence
o Mental Toughness
    - Positive
    - Enthusiastic
    - Confident in self
o Determination
    - Self-motivated
    - INTEGRITY
o Words and actions are in alignment
o Your actions meet your principles
o Disciplined enough to do what is right, even when others do not
    - SERVANT LEADERSHIP
o Selflessness
    - Do not let your teammates down

- Accept your role on the team—all roles are equal Enthusiasm
- SPORTSMANSHIP Respect the game
- Rules
- Opponent
- Officials
- Facilities
  o Perspective—"Compete as Christ would have competed"
  o Poise

The Team of Character Award is the most prestigious award that can be presented to your team. It encompasses every aspect of **GOLD PRIDE**.

Please use the following scale to rate your team:

3 Good
2 Average
1 Poor

Academic Excellence of Team
_____ Team GPA
_____ Class Attendance
_____ Grade Reports

Campus Leadership and Involvement
_____ Chapel attendance
_____ Attendance at VU athletic events
_____ Involvement in other VU campus groups (this would include how many on your team are LIONS)

Community Involvement
_____ Your evaluation of your team being involved as a team in the community

Embracing the Five Core Values

Respect

Teachable Spirit
_____ Ability to take instruction
_____ Dedicated to **pursuing excellence** (academically, athletically, character building)
_____ Team improvement during the season
_____ Desire to get an education and not just a degree
_____ Pursue the Vanguard University lifestyle standards

Work Habits
_____ Willing to be subjected to hard, productive work
_____ Willing to make the necessary sacrifices to be prepared to work diligently every day
_____ Committed to working hard to improve every area of your life
_____ Conscientious in getting everything done in a timely manner

Team Development

_____ Unselfishness
_____ Builds positive traditions
_____ Good leadership
_____ Trust
_____ Ownership of **GOLD PRIDE**—Significance

Responsibility

Consistency

_____ Reliable in every situation

Discipline

_____ Focus on pursuing excellence

Mental Toughness

_____ Positive
_____ Enthusiastic
_____ Confident in self

Determination

_____ Self-motivated

Integrity

_____ Words and actions are in alignment
_____ Your actions meet your principles
_____ Disciplined enough to do what is right, even when others do not

Servant Leadership

Selflessness

_____ Do not let your teammates down
_____ Accept your role on the team—all roles are equal
_____ Enthusiasm

Sportsmanship

Respect the Game
_____ Rules
_____ Opponent
_____ Officials
_____ Facilities
_____ Perspective: "Compete as Christ would have competed"
_____ Poise

Total Points: _____

Divide total points by 39: _____

Champions of Character
Team Award Score

CHAMPIONS OF CHARACTER
TEAM AWARD SCALE

3.0—2.5   GOLD—Meets the expecta-
           tions of past recipients
2.49—2.0   BLUE—Has improved in
           their character this past year
           but has not quite reached the
           GOLD LEVEL
1.99—below WHITE—Needs more
           improvement as a team of
           character

Endnotes

[1] James Maxwell. *The 17 Essential Qualities of A Team Player*. Nashville: Thomas Nelson, 1997, 107.
[2] James Maxwell. *The 17 Essential Qualities of A Team Player*. Nashville: Thomas Nelson, 1997, 24.
[3] James Maxwell. *The 17 Essential Qualities of A Team Player*. Nashville: Thomas Nelson, 1997, 24.
[4] James Maxwell. *The 17 Essential Qualities of A Team Player*. Nashville: Thomas Nelson, 1997, 110.
[5] James Maxwell. *The 17 Essential Qualities of A Team Player*. Nashville: Thomas Nelson, 1997, 111.
[6] James Maxwell. *The 17 Essential Qualities of A Team Player*. Nashville: Thomas Nelson, 1997, 114.
[7] James Maxwell. *The 17 Essential Qualities of A Team Player*. Nashville: Thomas Nelson, 1997, 111.
[8] James Maxwell. *The Winning Attitude*. Nashville: Thomas Nelson, 1997,165.
[9] James Maxwell. *The 17 Essential Qualities of A Team Player*. Nashville: Thomas Nelson, 1997, 145.
[10] James Maxwell. *Becoming a Person of Influence*. Nashville: Thomas Nelson, 1997, 49.
[11] Joe Ehrmann. *InsideOut Coaching*. New York: Simon and Schuster, 2011, 150.

Look What You Have Become

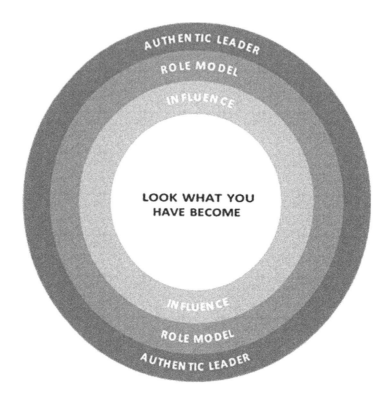

Audience of One

Galatians 2:20 reads, "I have been crucified with Christ; it is no longer I who live, but Christ lives in me; and the *life* which I now live in the flesh I live by faith in the Son of God, who loved me and gave Himself for me."

Influence

Role Model-Influencer

"A life is not significant except for its impact on other lives."
—Jackie Robinson

Many different people (role models) that have had a positive impact on your life never knew they made a difference. They gave you inspiration and carried you through difficult times. If this is true in your life you need to understand that you to have had an impact on others' lives. Everyone is a role model. The only question is whether you are a good or bad one. Role modeling is *The Ripple Effect* in action. Good role models are a blessing that lasts three lifetimes. Their positive effect is passed on to the next two generations. If you are out in the community, your community, or in the athletic arena you are being looked at. Whether you like it or not, the choices in behavior that you make are a reflection of you and have the potential to influence others. You have to be strong and consistent in your character. You never know who is watching as you live your dreams, but you do know that others are watching. They are not trying to catch you stubbing your toe. They are looking for inspiration, and they hope you will show them the way. You may be their hero, and it is important that you do not let them down. Your life will have an impact on many people whom you will never know. You want that impact to be positive. You want to make a positive difference in their life.

People are first influenced by what they see. Parents can attest to this statement. No matter what you tell your children to do, their natural inclination is to follow what they see you doing. For most people, if they perceive that you are positive and trustworthy and have admirable qualities, then they will seek you as an influencer (role model) in their lives. And the better they get to know you, the greater your credibility will be and the higher your influence can become—if they like what they see.

When you meet people who do not know you, at first you have no influence with them at all. If someone they trust introduces you to them and gives you an endorsement, then you can temporarily "borrow" some of that person's influence. They will assume that you are credible until they get to know you. But as soon as they have some time to observe you, you either build or bust that influence by your actions.

One interesting exception to this modeling process occurs in the case of celebrities. Because of society's preoccupation with television, movies, and the media, many people are strongly influenced by others that they have never met. More often than not, they are not influenced by the actual individual, but by the image of the person. And that may not be an accurate representation of that actress, politician, sports figure or entertainer. Nonetheless, they admire that person and are influenced by actions and attitudes they believe that person represents."[1]

Influence can be either positive or negative. Values have to be an integral part of a person's character and integrated in their actions. When values are authentic and flow out of a person's character and self-awareness as part of a lifestyle, they can be applied consistently and with integrity. The reality in athletics is that other people evaluate student athletes by watching you—watching how you treat them, your teammates, the opponents and the officials. No matter what your athletic ability is or how well you perform, they gauge your real value by your actions. Famous American poet-philosopher Ralph Waldo Emerson said, "Every man is a hero and an oracle to somebody, and to that person, whatever he says has enhanced value."

PUT YOUR PICTURE HERE

The world may mean very little, but to someone little you may mean the world.

ROLE MODEL
AN ATHLETE'S RESPONSIBILITY
You are a hero in someone's eyes
In you trust and honor lies
As an Athlete fit and strong
He feels you can do no wrong.
Because he wants to be like you
All your words are deemed as true,
All he sees and all he hears
Will surely guide him through the years.
Teach him courage and insight
To tell the truth and do what is
right, To deal with failure and it's
sting And attitude is everything.
The example you set each day
Will help send him on his way,
Through your virtue he will see
That you are the person he hopes to be

Matthew 5:13–16 says, "Let me tell you why you are here. You're here to be salt-seasoning that brings out the God-flavors of this earth. If you lose your saltiness, how will people taste godliness? You've lost your usefulness and will end up in the garbage." Another way to put it is: "You're here to be light, bringing out the God-colors in the world. God is not a secret to be kept. We're going public with this, as public as a city on a hill. If I make you light-bearers, you don't think I'm going to hide you under a bucket, do you? I'm putting you on a light stand. Now that I've put you there on a hilltop, on a light stand—shine! Keep open house; be generous with your lives. By opening up to others, you'll prompt people to open up with God, this generous Father in heaven."

Most of the time, you recognize the influence you have on those closest to you. However, you need to be cognizant of the influence you have on other people around you. "The anonymous author of this poem probably had that in mind when he wrote,

My life shall touch a dozen lives
before this day is done,
Leave countless marks for good
or ill ere sets the evening sun,
This is the wish I always wish,
the prayer I always pray;
Lord, may my life help other
lives it touches by the way.[2]

If you want to leave a legacy you will become a man or woman capable of influencing others. Larry Dobbs once said, "The only inheritance that a man will leave that has eternal value is his influence." You will choose from day to day or from situation to situation, what kind of influence you will be. This is the power you have to make a difference in the world around us. However, you need to understand that we all leave a legacy. The question is what kind of legacy you want to leave. This is not a question you should put off until your last days on earth. It is something you need to think about now. Do not worry about your platform; focus on the impact you can have. One way or another you will have a platform. God will supply that. How you use the opportunities you are given to affect the world around you will determine the legacy you leave behind. You need to focus on the impact you can have through your platform as a student athlete on adding value to people's lives. Not everyone will have the same impact; we all were created with different gifts and abilities. The real question is what you can do with the platform you have. It is the mind-set that sees the platform as it is—not as it someday may be—and takes action now. It is the mind-set that focuses on having a positive impact on others wherever they may be. Regardless of your situation in life, you are always role models for someone—always—and probably in ways you would not expect. Part of the beauty of role models is that you can find them in unexpected places, at unexpected times. You also need to realize that you may be unexpected role models for others.

"Influence does not come to us instantaneously. It grows by stages."[3] "No matter what your goals are in life or what you want to accomplish, you can achieve them faster, you can be more effective, and the contribution you make can be longer lasting if you learn how to become a person of influence."[4] Through your character development and spiritual formation have you implemented the "rules of the road" (core values) to maintain perspective and poise to do what is best and act correctly in making your choices that will not only affect you but influence others. In other words, are you real—authentic? Sometimes as a student athlete you become a selective participate when it comes to role modeling. You choose the situation that fits your agenda or time frame to be a role model but you do have not developed the discipline to be a consistent role model.

"You do not have to be in a high-profile occupation to be a person of influence. In fact, if your life in any way connects with other people, you are an influencer (role model)."[5] People who are role models know that they are, whether they like it or not. It is their behavior that people look up to. It is their leadership qualities that others want to see and model. It is the smile that they give to others. These people have developed the qualities to make choices that reflect their authenticity. Excellence is part of their lifestyle. Qualities that enhance the authenticity of a good role model include the following:

1. Having a positive outlook on life; being grateful of the difference of others.
2. Being courageous and taking the initiative; being considerate of their needs.
3. Being constructive with our words; being uncompromising, honest and caring
4. Being determined, focused, and ambitious.
5. Trusting God with your feelings.
6. Being confidential with information.
7. Being committed to relationships.
8. Making small commitments and keeping them.
9. Being a light—not a judge.
10. When you make a mistake admit it, correct it and learn from it.

11. Work on things you have control over.
12. Look at weaknesses of others with compassion, not accusation.

Influence is not measured on what you take up but what you give up. The Lakota warriors provide an excellent example of being a quality role model. These were fierce warriors but in their culture they did not bring attention to themselves in battle. They accepted their role and did their assignment. They sacrificed their personal rights and goals to help the group mission. If glory came to them as a result of being successful in battle they gave up their most prize possession to the group. This demonstrates humility and selflessness but also is a model of becoming authentic.

Today, I want to . . .
Write something worth reading
Read something worth sharing
Say something worth repeating
Give something worth getting
Choose something worth keeping
Sacrifice something worth giving up
Go somewhere worth seeing
Eat something worth tasting
Hug someone worth holding
Buy something worth treasuring
Cry tears worth shedding
Do something worth watching
Risk something worth protecting
Listen to something worth hearing
Teach something worth learning
Be someone worth knowing
Today, I want to be authentic

"Being a role model is the most powerful form of educating . . . too often fathers neglect it because they get so caught up in making a living they forget to make a life" (John Wooden).

Be the kind of man you'd like your son to become, the kind of man you would love your daughter to marry for life. Be the kind of woman you would like your daughter to be, the kind of woman you'd love your son to choose for a wife.

Stat Sheet

Fundamentals: Basic Skills

1. Role modeling is *The Ripple Effect* in action.
2. Whether you like it or not the choices in behavior that you make are a reflection of you and have the potential to influence others. You have to be strong and consistent in your character. You never know who is watching as you live your dreams, but you do know that others are watching.
3. If you want to leave a legacy you will become a man or woman capable of influencing others.
4. Know, understand, and use the ten word vocabulary.
5. Influence is not measured on what you take up but what you give up.

Strength and Conditioning Training: Improving Your Shape

It's only a quarter . . .

Several years ago, a preacher from out of state accepted a call to a church in Houston, Texas. Some weeks after he arrived, he had an occasion to ride the bus from his home to the downtown area. When he sat down, he discovered that the driver had accidentally given him a quarter too much change.

As he considered what to do, he thought to himself, you'd better give the quarter back. It would be wrong to keep it.' Then he thought, 'Oh, forget it, it's only a quarter. Who would worry about this little amount? Anyway, the bus company will never miss it. Accept it as 'a gift from God' and keep quiet.'

When his stop came, he paused momentarily at the door, and then he handed the quarter to the driver and said, 'Here, you gave me too much change.'

The driver, with a smile, replied, "Aren't you the new preacher in town? I have been thinking a lot lately about going somewhere to worship. I just wanted to see what you would do if I gave you too much change. I'll see you at church on Sunday."

When the preacher stepped off the bus, he literally grabbed the nearest light pole, held on, and said, "Oh, God, I almost sold your Son for a quarter."

Our lives are the only Bible some people will ever read. This is a really scary example of how much people watch us as Christians and will put us to the test! Always be on guard and remember that you carry the name of Christ on your shoulders when you call yourself "Christian."

Watch your thoughts; they become words.
Watch your words; they become actions.
Watch your actions; they become habits.
Watch your habits, they become character.
Watch your character; it becomes your destiny.

The college experience is not a vacation from responsibility; it is the training ground to become role models who dare to be responsible now.

Influence

1. How are you using your athletic platform to *influence* your team, teammates, be a role model or mentor leader?

Game Day: Performing with Excellence

Student athletes have a great platform of influence and have an impact as a role model.

Matthew 5:13–16

"[13]You are the salt of the earth; but if the salt loses its flavor, how shall it be seasoned? It is then good for nothing but to be thrown out and trampled underfoot by men. 14 "You are the light of the world. A city that is set on a hill cannot be hidden. 15 Nor do they light a lamp and put it under a basket, but on a lamp stand, and it gives light to all who are in the house. 16 Let your light so shine before men, that they may see your good works and glorify your Father in heaven."

Through *The Ripple Effect* process, you have had an opportunity to think through what defines you (your identity), been involved in in-depth discussion of what **GOLD PRIDE** is all about and how that can make you a better teammate for your team. Given this knowledge how will you represent **GOLD PRIDE**?

Endnotes

[1] James Maxwell. *Becoming a Person of Influence*. Nashville: Thomas Nelson, 1997, 6–7.
[2] James Maxwell. *Becoming a Person of Influence*. Nashville: Thomas Nelson, 1997, 10.
[3] James Maxwell. *Becoming a Person of Influence*. Nashville: Thomas Nelson, 1997, 5.
[4] James Maxwell. *Becoming a Person of Influence*. Nashville: Thomas Nelson, 1997, 3.
[5] James Maxwell. *Becoming a Person of Influence*. Nashville: Thomas Nelson, 1997, 3.

Authentic Leader

Authentic leadership is all about being a servant leader.

Jesus said, "For even the Son of Man came not to be served but to serve others and to give His life as a ransom for many."
—Mark 10:45

Part of the purpose of life is to build a legacy—a consistent pattern of building into the lives of others with wisdom, experience, and loyalty that can be passed on to succeeding generations. Building a life of significance, and creating a legacy of real value, means being willing to step out in your life and onto the platform of influence you have been given and touch the lives of people in need. Authentic leaders build authentic leaders.

Nobel prize winning author, Alexander Solzhenitsyn noted, "The meaning of earthly existing lies, not as we have grown used to thinking, in prospering, but in the development of the soul. The development of character is at the heart of our development not just as leaders, but as human beings."[1]

One competency stands alone in authentic leadership and it is character. As critically important as a shared vision is for leadership, character is even more fundamental and essential. Authentic leadership is character and spiritual formation in action. Character is not a function or product of style. Character resides in one's spirit and the right leadership spirit is a product of the heart. From the heart flow moral courage, conviction and consciences as well as compassion. An authentic leader has the right combination of confidence and humility to recognize strengths and weaknesses and to consciously seek to build character, competency, nurture spiritual formation, and confidence of those they are leading. A leader with the right style may be able to get people to do what needs to be done, but a leader whose focus is on spirit as well as style can motivate people to want do what needs to be done.

The real power and energy of a leader focusing on spirit rests in the relationship that develops for both the leader and the follower to commonly held set of values and objectives instead of merely the relationship of the leader to the follower. Character is the foundation on which all leadership is built. "Research has shown that in times of crisis, people gravitate toward the person with the highest character, not necessarily the person who is in charge or even the person they believe is the most competent. In a crisis people crave character. Character is the glue that bonds solid and meaningful relationships."[2]

Authentic leadership attributes include the following traits: demonstrating courage and leading by example, keeping others focused, while demonstrating faith, and being willing to evaluate yourself when change is needed. A leader must be courageous to make and stick with choices or decisions that are made for the good of the team. In leading by example you must be an example of what the team stands for. As the leader you should be the first to be accountable to the standards of the team. "I have given you an example to follow. "Now do as I have done to you" (John 13:15). "Don't lord it over the people assigned to your care, but lead them by your good example (1 Peter 5:3). "Set an example for the believers in speech, in life, in love, in faith and in purity (integrity)" (1 Timothy 4:12). Bruce Brown in his booklet, Seven Ways To Lead A Team, Be First . . . Be Last" provides these ideas to model (be an example):

1. Be an example of ATTITUDE
   • The first to have a team attitude and the last to lose it.

2. Be an example of a TEACHABLE SPIRIT
   • Learn to take correction as a compliment
   • Eye contact and body language during correction

3. Be an example of POISE
   • Controlling your actions in times of emotion

4. Be an example of WORK ETHIC
   • First to arrive—last to leave

5. Be an example of EXCELLENCE
   • Great leaders have a hunger for not just success, but also for excellence.
   • Every decision should be measured against a shared vision of excellence that the team and coach possess.

6. Be an example of ACCOUNTABILITY
   • Accountability is reliability for the work that must be done.

7. Be an example of INITIATIVE
   • Be the first to see and take action for what needs to be done and be the last one who avoids work.

An authentic leader encourages and communicates with people on an emotional level. "This creates a bridge between you and them; it builds up their sense of confidence and self-worth. When people feel good about you and themselves during the times they are with you, then your level of influence increases significantly."[3] People with positive role models have something to live for, somebody who is proud of them, somebody who cares about their well-being. Authentic leadership is about building character into the lives of others. To nurture you must be a giver. "The length and breadth of our influence on others is directly related to the depth of our concern for them."[4] To nurture others these qualities need to be present: love, respect, sense of security, recognition and encouragement. "When love focuses on giving to others, respect shows a willingness to receive from them. Respect acknowledges another person's ability or potential to contribute."[5]

Nurturing is building faith in them. Giving people, a sense of security is extremely important. "People are reluctant to trust you and reach their potential when they are worried about whether they are safe with you . . . part of making people feel secure comes from integrity . . . people feel secure with you when your actions and words are consistent and conform to a high moral code that includes respect."[6] Trust and respect allow others to believe in you; to have faith in you. There are far too many people today that do not believe in themselves for a variety of reasons. They do not have confidence in themselves, they believe they will fail and therefore, lack faith both in themselves and in a higher authority because they believe they are not good enough for God. "They see difficulty in every possibility. But the reality is that difficulties seldom defeat people; lack of faith in themselves usually does."[7] "When you have faith in others, you give them an incredible gift. Give others money, and it is soon spent. Give resources, and they may not be used to their best advantage. Give help, and people will often find themselves back where they started in short period of time. But give them you faith, and they become confident, energized, and self-reliant."[8]

When a person is encouraged, they can face the impossible and overcome incredible adversity. When you nurture people, they receive several things that include positive self-worth, a sense of belonging, perspective, a feeling of significance, and hope. "The primary focus of authentic leadership is to shape the lives of the people right in front of you, to lead, guide, inspire and encourage those people."[9] Thus, teaching attitudes and behaviors; creating a constructive legacy to be passed along to future generations of leaders.

An authentic leader shepherds people. The first principle in shepherding others is to know them. As a leader you cannot lead what you do not know. You need to encourage them on a regular basis. You need to have a valid interest in them and work with them on a one on one basis. They are individuals and that is exactly how they want to be treated. You need to discover their skills and interests. You need to know their goals and dreams; what motivates them; what are their ambitions; what frustrates them? They need to know how much you care.

Authentic leadership is about relationships, integrity, and developing spiritual formation. Success is measured in changed lives, strong character and eternal values rather than in material gain, temporal achievement or status. Authentic leadership is pouring your life into other people and helping them reach their potential. It is about serving God by serving others. That is the mind-set of the authentic leader. You need to identify and develop the qualities that allow you to become a quality authentic leader. These qualities of an authentic leader should direct and guide everything you do and you should develop them prayerfully as you move forward. In doing so you can create a legacy of faith, hope and love that will outlive you and make a difference in the world (ripple effect).

"I was walking in the park and this guy waved at me. Then he said, I am sorry, I thought you were someone else. 'I said, I am'"

—Demetri Martin

"When someone accepts Christ, he becomes a brand new person inside. He is not the same anymore. A new life has begun! (2 Corinthians 5:17).

Jesus loves you in spite of what you know about yourself. It is not who you are but what God says about you. Nothing shapes you into the person you were created to be like the love of Christ. Religion is about you attempting to prove yourself to God and is based on performance. Relationship with Christ is about what God has done for you. Jesus exists to prove God's love for you—He pursues you in love because you cannot get there by yourself. Luke 3:22–23 demonstrates God's love for His son Jesus, "After all the people were baptized, Jesus was baptized. As He was praying, the sky opened up and the Holy Spirit, like a dove descending, came down on Him. And along with the Spirit, a voice: "You are my Son, chosen and marked by my love, pride of my life." This was God's love for His son Jesus and He has the same unconditional love for you, a love that empowers, shapes, transforms, and sets you free and brings you closer to God so you can endure anything. God's love is perfect. God's love erases the boundaries of what is impossible in your life. Seek Him, His love allows you to become the person you want to be and to live the life you want to live because it shapes you into an role model, authentic leader, ultimate competitor that God want you to become using your gifts and talents for Him.

In the development of character and spiritual formation, you tend to look at how far you need to go instead of looking at how far you have come. Character and spiritual formation are synonymous. God tests those He intends to use. God is more interested in your character than your performance. On the cross Jesus did not say, "I am not going to do this if you do not believe, He said I am going to do this because I love you." Nails did not hold Jesus to the cross it was love; His love for you to pay for your sins. Jesus power is different because He never stops loving you. The questions is do you trust Him enough through your faith to believe in His power. Jesus may surprise you but He will never disappoint you; because Jesus character is love; to be an ultimate competitor, compete for an audience of one, you need to keep your eyes focused on Jesus. You need to see yourself as God sees you not how the world sees you.

The Ripple Effect process has brought each of you into community by coming, working, thinking, and believing together and through the application of the rules of the road, you have experience a deeper understanding of who you are, whose you are, developed what is important to you and developed priorities so that you can move toward obtaining your potential through the discovery of the power of Christ and use this knowledge in a plan that develops empathy, strives for excellence and emulates Christ from the sidelines to the sidewalks to significance. **GOLD PRIDE** in action!

Your biggest battle in life is with yourself. If you want something you have never had before you must be willing to do something you have never done before. God does the deepest work in your life on your identity.

"Pride is all about me (ego), but confidence is a realization that God has given you abilities and created you to fill a unique role that no one else is called to fill. Confidence with humility is a recognition life is not about you but using the gifts and talents you have been blessed with to their fullest. And it is not using gifts to benefit you, but to help your team and impact others . . . It is embracing the idea that God created you for a particular place and time and sharing that your life with others who were also created to play a role. Once you can do that, it becomes much easier to let go of status and false ideas of respect."[10] "Character and faith are tested, revealed, and further developed by the decisions you make in the most challenging times; character reflects a life committed to uncompromising integrity. Albert Camus once said, 'Integrity has no rules.'"[11] You and you alone determine if you will be a person of character and grow spiritually.

You need to look for faith in order to live the life you should. Faith is believing in what is true. Faith has two elements: (1) being convinced of the truth, being certain of reality, having evidence of unseen things; and (2) believing, hoping in, embracing, seizing the truth. The fundamental fact of existence is that this trust in God, this faith, is the firm foundation under everything that makes life worth living. It is our handle on what you cannot see.

While faith requires being convinced that what you believe in is true, just knowing the truth is only half of faith. God's word must be hoped for, embraced, seized! Real faith is about Jesus. Real faith is about following Jesus. Following after Christ is a journey just as your collegiate experience is a journey. We all travel in herds, Jesus asks you to go away from the herd and then the herd criticizes you for doing so, so you go back to the herd. We need to decide to live in the light of eternity, not the here and now. During your character development and spiritual formation there will be tests that will require trusting Jesus. Jesus learned to become obedient through hard times; just as you have done as a student athlete. To walk with Jesus, you need to trust Him and to trust Him and you need to put your trust in His timing. Jesus does not operate on your time schedule. Jesus timing is unique be the fact remains that He never stops loving you.

During your character and faith journey you will have different thoughts and experience, as well as many different feelings and emotions. Sometimes you may feel unworthy of the presence of God's in your life. Christ was perfect and you are not; do not try to feel worthy but merely except the fact that Jesus made you worthy by what He did for you on the cross. During your faith walk there will be times of doubt as well as struggles and sometimes failure. In doubt be courageous and just admit your doubt, work and talk through it with others. During struggles look to strengthen a relationship with Jesus and with others; the only way to have great relationships is to have a power outside you. During times where you feel you have let yourself, your teammates or God down you need to refocus. Refocus on the love of Jesus. Be disappointed in falling short but not discouraged, turn your focus to the basics of your faith—get into God's word and finally strengthen yourself by getting in the company of others who will support and encourage you.

The Ripple Effect is a process of moving from success to significance to surrender. Dallas Willard suggests this process includes the following, "the first step is a struggle, which is trying to be successful; the second is success, which means you have reached that point, and I believe that in today's world most people can achieve a level of success if they have focus and determination. The third is significance, which I define . . . using your experience and knowledge to help others. And finally, comes surrender, which means being fully aligned with a higher purpose for your life."[12]

To receive God's blessing you need to be willing to let go, surrender; to surrender in spirituality, you completely give up your own will and subject your thoughts, ideas, and deeds to the will and teachings of a higher power. You need to express trust in God's wisdom. God will touch you at your strongest points to remind you to depend on His strength. You win struggles with God by surrendering. In **surrendering** to God you let go of the security you have, the things you value and the people you hold precious. You must let go of your comfort zone, your culture and traditions, and relationship. Thus, you clear out space in your life so you can receive God's blessings. Spiritual breathing, breathe out sin and garbage, breathe in God's power. Willard further describes his thoughts concerning significance and surrender indicating "that significance actually requires surrender. I do not think you can really manage surrender within the parameters of

success; you have to give up. You have to surrender yourself to this other good before you can achieve the kind of significance we are talking about. If you set your sights on attaining that final step of surrender and give yourself up to being a blessing to others, which is the source of significance."[13] "The critical difference between success and significance is that success has more to do with outcomes, I am in charge of, while significance has more to do with outcomes I am not in charge of. The beautiful thing about significance is that we resign the outcomes to God, and we let a power beyond ourselves take care of them. Success is focused on my action, my control, my outcomes, whereas significance is found in a much larger context. I am not running that context, and the step of surrender is critical because surrender allows me to release the outcome."[14] Mark 8:36–37 says, "And what do you benefit if you gain the whole world, but lose your own soul? Is anything worth more than your soul?" In surrendering your security, your current culture and traditions, and your relationships you are beginning to move toward significance and put yourself in a position to receive God's blessings as an authentic leader—ultimate competitor.

"Do not you realize that in a race everyone runs, but only one person gets the prize? So run to win! All athletes are disciplined in their training. They do it to win a prize that will fade away, but we do it for an eternal prize. So I run with purpose in every step. I am not just shadowboxing. I discipline my body like an athlete, training it to do what it should." (1 Corinthians 9:24–27). What race are you running, your race or God's?

God has a plan for your life but you need to look for that plan. God loved you before you were born. God has given each of you grace and mercy to use your gifts and talents to run His race for your life.

What happens when you get into Jesus boat? God will bless you with a new direction, new relationships, and begin to help you develop and build a legacy. You will become a Christian Athlete with a purpose. The greatest use of your life is to invest it in something that will outlast it. As a Christian Athlete you will become a kingdom builder. Kingdom builders that reach significance have the purpose of God, the plan of God, and the will of God in their lives.

Being an Ultimate Competitor gives you a new identity. You do not base your identity on something you can lose—God's unconditional love cannot be taken from you. You need to see yourself as God sees you, not how the world lies to you. We feel pressured to tie our personal value to our ability as an athlete. Too often, we believe that our value is determined solely by our achievements and is measured against the standards of our sport that pays homage to winning or success. You get a false identity from your relationships, your sport, your environment or things (bling). God's will for your life is revealed in Romans 12:2: "Let God transform you into a new person by changing the way you think. Then you will know what God wants for you to do, His good, pleasing and perfect for your life."

Make God the foundation of your life; you are not living if you do not love God and others. Always remember what matters most; love matters most. Galatians 5:6b says, "The only thing that counts is faith expressing itself through love." Your destiny is determined by your relationships. Become a great teammate; your appetite is influenced by your associations; do you make your teammates better; do your teammates make you a better person. **Commit yourself to a great purpose.** The secret of greatness is when an ordinary person commits to a great cause because it brings out greatness in them. Finally, **have the courage to stand alone. Learn to lead the crowd**; "do not join any crowd that intends to do evil…and do not be swayed in your testimony by the opinion of the majority" (Exodus 23:2). **Be willing to do what others will not.** "Stand true to what you believe. Be courageous. Be strong. And everything you do must be done in love" (1 Corinthians 16:13–14). **Be willing to live differently.** "An honorable person acts honestly and stands firm for what is right" (Isaiah 32:8). **Remember following Christ is courageous—fitting in is not.** You need to understand the significance of your choices and do what is right. **Fear the disapproval of God more than the approval of society.** This is *The Ripple Effect to Develop Character and Spiritual Formation.*

"I pray that Christ will be more and more at home in your hearts as you trust Him. May your roots go down deep into the soil of God's marvelous love. And I pray you will be able to feel and understand how long, how wide, how deep and how high God's love for you really is; and to experience His love for yourself, though it is so great you will never fully understand it" (Ephesians 3:18–19). The greatest ability is dependability. Being a competitor is not dependent on your gender, your sport or your genetics. Being a competitor is a choice, it is a decision and it becomes a lifestyle. Competitors anticipate the great feelings that comes with succeeding by having that be their focus. They enjoy the journey as much as the result. Sometimes the fear of losing causes people to become competitive because they see losing as failure; these athletes usually find themselves competing not to lose and they sacrifice the natural joy of competing because their focus is on the final score. The ultimate competitor sees competition as an enjoyable component of life by keeping their focus on the positive aspects. They compete for an audience of one.

Being an Ultimate Competitor gives you a new ability; power, strength, energy. God works in you through the Holy Spirit. "Therefore, since we have been justified through faith, we have peace with God through our Lord Jesus Christ, through whom we have gained access by faith into this grace in which we now stand. And we boast in the hope of the glory of God. Not only so, but we also glory in our sufferings, because we know that suffering produces perseverance; perseverance, character; and character, hope. And hope does not put us to shame, because God's love has been poured out into our hearts through the Holy Spirit, who has been given to us" (Romans 5:1–5). We all have desire but not ability, the Holy Spirit gives us the ability; the power to start over when we have blown it; the power to get through it—to stay with it; the power to sustain so we can obtain significance.

Being an Ultimate Competitor makes you a better teammate. "We never know for sure how long God will give us with the people we love."[15]

Nowhere in our lives is the tension greater than in the area of setting priorities that matter most. A compelling and distorted perception in our society today is that respect comes from status, achievements and success. In other words, we believe the myth that style is more important than substance. "Somewhere we have lost the concept that respect comes from appreciating who a person is inside and what he is truly all about. We do not respect the man; we respect what he does or what he has. The real danger here is that choosing style over substance keeps us from valuing those things that truly do have worth."[16] "I am sure that God, who began a good work within you, will continue his work until it is finally finished on that day when Christ Jesus comes back again" (Philippians 1:6). Jesus will complete your character development to bring you to completion to be like Christ; to live your life with significance and live the way you are meant to be live by choosing substance over style and **TO BECOME AN ULTIMATE COMPETITOR**.

"Do your best, prepare for the worst—then trust GOD to bring victory."
(Proverbs 21:31MSG)

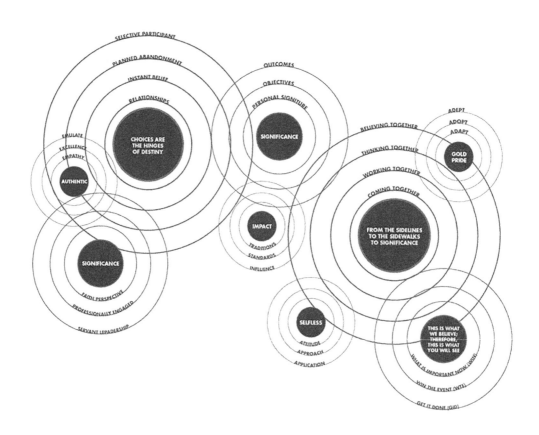

Be careful how you speak to yourself;
Be careful how you think of yourself;
Be careful of how you conduct yourself;
Be careful of how you develop yourself.
—Tony Dungy

Your choices have influenced your destiny and put you on the path to significance.

This Is the Ripple Effect

One student athlete with Christian character can improve a team
One team with Christian character can improve an athletic program
One athletic program with Christian character can impact a community
From the sideline, to the sidewalk, to significance

GOLD PRIDE

CHERISH EACH DAY AND OPPORTUNITY

Senior reflection from Tennis Seniors Gabrielle Alford and Roger Muri

Roger: I cherished the moment I got accepted to Vanguard.

Gabrielle: I cherished every time I had the chance to gain spiritual growth in chapel, in the classroom, and with all my teammates.

Roger: I cherished every time I had the opportunity to gain knowledge in the classroom.

Gabrielle: I cherished the many early mornings on the tennis court.

Roger: I cherished every road trip with my teammates.

Gabrielle: I cherished all the possibilities I had to be as good as my God given talent allowed me to be.

Roger: I cherished the bond between teammates that no one can take away from us.

Gabrielle: I cherished the support and knowledge our coach shared with us all.

Roger: I cherished every servant leadership project we did.

Gabrielle: I cherished the very unique times we had when reaching out to underprivileged kids in the deep south at the National Championship.

Roger: I cherished the bonding with all the students and athletes on campus.

Gabrielle: I cherished all of the encouraging words from teachers and coaches of other sports.

Roger: I cherished the blessings of Bob Wilson—the best leader in NAIA.

Gabrielle: I cherished the countless hours in the athletic training room with the wonderful trainers.

Roger: I cherished the appreciated work of Diane, Nolan, and Jeff who make everything happen.

Gabrielle: I cherished my dear teammates, coaches, the entire athletic department and all of you other athletes sitting in this room tonight.

Roger: All these cherished moments are something I wish all my teammates could have experienced and it hurts me deeply and

I am heartbroken that they will never have the same beautiful memories as me.

Gabrielle: As much as I always will cherish Vanguard athletics, coaches, teachers, and all of you . . . athletes, a piece of my heart died when finding out my teammates will never be able to cherish all these wonderful moments.

Roger: I ask all of you athletes to cherish every minute of every day and every practice because time will fly by quickly.

Gabrielle: and you will never be sure everything will end the way in which you have dreamt.

God blesses you every day. The nicest place to be is in someone's thoughts. The safest place to be is in someone's prayers, and the very best place to be is. . . In the hands of God.

God believes in you more than you think and God's plan for you is bigger than you believe.

—JOHNNIE MOORE

Stat Sheet

Fundamentals: Basic Skills

1. The secret to growth in character and spiritual formation is continual evaluation and assessment. Test yourself to make sure you are solid in your faith.
   - What have you learned through the ripple effect about character development and spiritual formation?

Strength and Conditioning Training: Improving Your Shape

1. Character growth and your spiritual formation do not come from rules but from small actions of responsibility that occur daily. It is more important to pursue the hard right (doing the correct thing), instead of the easy wrong. When it is all said and done, your reputation does not matter. It is important, but what others think of you is simply out of your control. What does matter, however, is what you think of yourself.
   a. How would others describe your reputation today?
   b. Has **GOLD PRIDE** helped to improve your reputation?
   c. How has the lens of how you view your collegiate experience changes from learning about **GOLD PRIDE**?
   d. Will you become an authentic leader?

2. Competition can be defined as a mutual quest or striving for excellence. It is more process oriented than outcome oriented. Competitors strive together or with each other to bring out the best by presenting a worthy challenge. Competition, therefore, is not defined by winning and losing, but by the degree to which all competitors realize their fullest potential. Since true competition is a "mutual quest for excellence" there are no winners or losers; everyone who competes wins. This cooperative sense of competition is a value-driven process that leads to; respect for others—your teammates and your opponent; personal and team integrity; being the best you are capable of becoming instead of, doing whatever it takes to get ahead and win. Your self-worth is never determined by winning or losing. Our desire to dominate an opponent is a result of insecurity, a sense of insignificance, and shame. Competitors can be after the same goal—excellence but they cannot find it alone. The relationship among opponents should be built upon respect for each other, the game, the rules and the honor of competition. True competition, is about maintaining the honor of the opponent. We want to win and play to win, but never at the expense of the opponent's well-being. Competition is not about winning or perfection. It entails being

the best you are capable of becoming based on your unique gifts, talents, and abilities. We compete with others to achieve excellence, but the person you become in the pursuit of excellence is worth far more than the apparent achievement of excellence.

- How has the *The Ripple Effect of Character Development and Spiritual Formation* changed your thoughts on competition?

Game Day: Performing with Excellence

1. On a scale of 1 to 5 with 5 being the highest value, how would you rate yourself on being an Ultimate Competitor (competing for an audience of one) at this time in your collegiate experience? Why?
2. Will you become an authentic leader?

Endnotes

1 James Maxwell. *The 21 Indispensable Qualities of a Leader*. Nashville: Thomas Nelson, 1999, 4.
2 Tony Dungy. *The Mentor Leader, Secrets To Build People and Teams That Win Consistently*. Tyndale House Publishers, Inc. 2010, 71.
3 James Maxwell. *Becoming a Person of Influence*. Nashville: Thomas Nelson, 1997, 7.
4 James Maxwell. *Becoming a Person of Influence*. Nashville: Thomas Nelson, 1997, 41.
5 James Maxwell. *Becoming a Person of Influence*. Nashville: Thomas Nelson, 1997, 43.
6 James Maxwell. *Becoming a Person of Influence*. Nashville: Thomas Nelson, 1997, 43–44.
7 James Maxwell. *Becoming a Person of Influence*. Nashville: Thomas Nelson, 1997, 62.
8 James Maxwell. *Becoming a Person of Influence*. Nashville: Thomas Nelson, 1997, 64–65.
9 Tony Dungy. *The Mentor Leader, Secrets To Build People and Teams That Win Consistently*. Tyndale House Publishers, Inc. 2010, XVI.
10 Tony Dungy. *Finding Your Path To Significance Uncommon*. Tyndale House Publishers, Inc.2009, 19–20.
11 Tony Dungy. *Finding Your Path To Significance Uncommon*. Tyndale House Publishers, Inc.2009, 7.
12 Bob Buford. *Finishing Well*. Zondervan, 2004, 14.
13 Bob Buford. *Finishing Well*. Zondervan, 2004, 14.
14 Bob Buford. *Finishing Well*. Zondervan, 2004, 18.
15 Tony Dungy. *Finding Your Path To Significance Uncommon*. Tyndale House Publishers, Inc.2009, 153.
16 Tony Dungy. *Finding Your Path To Significance Uncommon*. Tyndale House Publishers, Inc.2009, 148.

About the Author

Bob Wilson has been deeply committed to making a significant impact on students and student athletes. He has used the platform of athletics to teach competitive excellence in academics, athletics, and character building. His career in collegiate athletics has spanned forty-eight years. He recently retired as the athletic director at Vanguard University after twenty-one years. He coached basketball at the collegiate level for more than twenty-four years.

He has a bachelor of science degree from Wyoming University in biological science and masters of arts from the University of Nebraska at Omaha in physical education. While at Wyoming, Bob met his wife, Tammy Eckhardt, who is retired from teaching special education for thirty-six years. They have been married for forty-eight years and have two daughters Saundi and Nikki and five grandchildren.

Bob Wilson has dedicated his career to competitive excellence. Competitive excellence is not defined by winning and losing, but by the degree to which all competitors realize their fullest potential. The reason for competition is to have a result. However, the most important element for those that participate in the competition is to win with honor, lose with dignity, and compete with character.

Wilson served on the NAIA Champions of Character Advisory Committee from 2005 until his retirement and is certified by the NAIA as a Champions of Character Instructor. He spends a great deal of time speaking in the community about changing the culture of sport. As part of Vanguard's program center, he created the University's Gold Pride program to personalize and conceptualize the Champions of Character initiative on the VU campus. Through the implementation of this program, he developed the curriculum, provide the instruction, and wrote *The Ripple Effect* for the character class offered to all new Vanguard student athletes.

9 781641 403382